The Wee Wild One

Irish Studies in Literature and Culture

MICHAEL PATRICK GILLESPIE

SERIES EDITOR

The Wee Wild One

Stories of Belfast and Beyond

Ruth Schwertfeger

THE UNIVERSITY OF WISCONSIN PRESS

The University of Wisconsin Press
1930 Monroe Street
Madison, Wisconsin 53711

www.wisc.edu/wisconsinpress/

3 Henrietta Street
London WC2E 8LU, England

Printed in the United States of America

Library of Congress Cataloging-in-Publication Data
Schwertfeger, Ruth.
The wee wild one: stories of Belfast and beyond / Ruth C. Schwertfeger.
p.   cm.—(Irish studies in literature and culture)
Includes bibliographical references.
ISBN 0-299-19880-4 (cloth: alk. paper)
1. Belfast (Northern Ireland)—Social life and customs.
2. Schwertfeger, Ruth—Homes and haunts—Northern Ireland—Belfast.
3. College teachers—United States—Biography.
4. Northern Ireland—Social life and customs.
5. Schwertfeger, Ruth—Childhood and youth.
6. Belfast (Northern Ireland)—Biography.
7. Irish American women—Biography.
8. Northern Ireland—Biography.   9. Schwertfeger, Ruth—Family.
10. Family—Northern Ireland.   I. Title.   II. Series.
DA995.B5S35   2004
941.6′70823′092—dc22   2003020578

Dedicated to my brother,
ALEX,
and to the memory of our sister,
ROSEMARY CULLEN

This is my home and country. Later on perhaps I'll find this nation is my own but here and now it is enough to love this faulted ledge, this map of cloud above, and the great sea that beats against the west to swamp the sun.

John Hewitt, from "Conacre"

L'accent du pays où l'on est né demeure dans l'esprit et dans le coeur, comme dans le langage.
[The accent of the country where you were born remains as much in your spirit and soul as in your language.]

La Rochefoucauld

Contents

Preface

The source of this book is to be found in the hills around Belfast where I spent my childhood. Its shape and telling are more recent tributaries yet still connected to the same stream. Several years ago, when already into my fifties and long since a permanent resident of the United States, I contributed a small piece to a commemorative history of my school in Belfast that was being edited by a former headmistress of the school. I responded to the request mostly out of affection for the teacher, who had joined the school staff toward the very end of my school days. After I had finished the little piece, however, I kept on writing. What was emerging were narratives that were a hybrid of essay and memoir—non-Proustian essay-memoirs, if you want me to be technical about the genre. For the sake of sanity, however, I'll refer to them simply as "stories."

Admittedly, I had already been writing for years but not about my native land and certainly not about myself. My focus was on other issues and other places, like Theresienstadt in the former Czechoslovakia, the "model" ghetto that interned more than 138,000 Jews between November 1941 and May 1945, before sending more than 88,000 of them to extermination camps in Poland. I was writing about women like Else Lasker-Schüler, the German-Jewish poet who survived the Holocaust but died heartbroken in exile in Jerusalem. So it was a great surprise to discover that writing under pressure for tenure and promotion had not totally depleted me—there might still be a few seams left to mine. It was surely worth exploring.

I should have understood sooner that such a pursuit was possible because Anne Crone, my mentor at school in Belfast, not only taught French and German but also wrote three novels. Over the years, however, I had buried the memory of her influence, had made my own way, and had not bothered to read her novels with adult eyes. Therefore, it came as a shock when I found her name on an American university website syllabus for Irish Studies. Anne Crone? My French and German teacher on the website of Irish Studies? If she were still living, would this intensely private woman object to such public exposure? Or would she too have joined the ranks of Irish women like Nuala O'Faolain, who are writing about themselves?

When I first discovered memoirs written by academic women, I was amazed that they had ever found time to write them. I experienced a certain reckless pleasure in reading them, especially when piles of student papers lay neglected on my desk. Of course, not all the memoirs I read were by women, but the strange thing is that as much as I responded to the memoirs about Ireland, I was more drawn to the memoirs of women who worked in my own field—women like the Germanist Ruth Klüger and the French professor Alice Kaplan.

I discovered the memoir of Ruth Klüger—*Weiter Leben*—in the summer of 1994 when I was teaching at the Justus Liebig Universität in Gießen. It had been given to me in that supercasual way that frequently prefaces a significant discovery: "I think this will interest you." Nothing in Klüger's post-Auschwitz memoir resonated with my own life thus far, and certainly I found no shared experience of a tortured mother-daughter relationship. But something in the way she told her story captivated me, especially the boldness in making the genre conform to her voice and not the other way around. Klüger's raw parenthetical comments are indeed intrusions on the narrative voice and disconnect her memoir from the genre, but what emerges is a text that is free and honest. Both Klüger and Kaplan, already distinguished scholars in their respective fields, opened doors to their lives far beyond the classroom and embraced these experiences as a vital part of their identity.

Yet I have a different story to tell, and my own native tongue to tell it in, including the irritating habit of repeating a point, which we have polished to an art in the north of Ireland. So we have. The genre that I use is not in the line of practitioners of the Irish memoir but draws instead from the models I have mentioned, as well as those that are more closely related to the essay form. I spent my childhood writing essays. It seemed an awful waste of daylight at the time. The teachers in our school in Belfast trained us to fit our lives, and the lives of everybody else remotely near us, into the essay. If it didn't fit an essay, it was not worth telling—that was the impression. The models they used to perfect the art were Hazlitt and Lamb—in other words, elderly Englishmen.

As a matter of routine we had to practice the skill on every school event that touched our lives; the most insignificant and dull event was deemed worthy of an essay. It was to be good training for what lay ahead. Thus an excursion to the Scrabo Tower near Comber with the geography teacher found its way into an essay, with all the prerequisites: the number of the local bus that we traveled on, an analysis of the local loam, detailed description of the type of vegetable gardening found on this fertile peninsula, finally the obligatory mention of the return journey on the bus. (As if we all had walked home or had disappeared without trace.) So in a sense these stories are also essays, submitted admittedly late and without teacher supervision, but they do fulfill the requirement for detail and can promise a safe return home.

Much later in my life I discovered the exemplary essay-story "Der Ausflug der toten Mädchen" (The Excursion of the Dead Girls) by the German Jewish writer Anna Seghers. In "The Excursion of the Dead Girls," Seghers returns to her native Germany by way of an essay that she volunteered to write about a day trip that she and her classmates had taken on the Rhine. I suppose that every class trip ever taken in the history of education exacts a price tag—in our case we *all* had to write about it, but in Seghers's story someone had to volunteer to describe what happened, and she was the one to do so. But the essay—story that she wrote was to come much later-in involuntary exile in Mexico (where she and her family found refuge after fleeing from Nazi Germany in 1933, first to Switzerland, then to France). The characters are the same in the book as in the essay, except that they are no longer girls on a school trip but grown women who made choices that aligned them with either Nazi ideology or the Resistance. In Seghers's story time present and time past intersect in the same sentence in stunning fusion and simultaneity. In the frame of the present tense in exile she is slowly recuperating from injuries sustained in a serious car accident while dealing at the same time with the terrible news that had reached her in Mexico City—her mother had perished in one of the camps of the East. In the frame of the past context she is still enjoying the view of her beloved Mainz from the deck of a little steamer on the Rhine, carefree and happy with

her girlfriends, all of them returning home in the slant-
ing light of the sun to loving families. Seghers's mother
is also waiting for her on the balcony. But the present
interrupts her narration; the schoolgirl's outstretched
arms fail to reach her waiting mother. In the end all the
girls are gone. Exhausted, she returns to the frame of
the story—still in exile, still in Mexico.

What I admire most in this story is Seghers's carefully controlled depiction of loss that she presents
in the same breath as her undisguised love for her native Rhineland. I invoke it at this point because I too
love the place where I was born and raised. I too left
my home—my *Heimat*—though certainly not chased
away, as was Seghers from Nazi Germany. She later
spoke in exile about lining up words—one alongside
the other—in order to preserve her native language. As
my ties to the province become loosened by the loss of
family members, it is through language, through local
dialect and colloquialisms, that I retain my connection
to the *Heimat*. Language helps me unlock the gate to
the past, to a time when my relationship to Northern
Ireland was still unfettered by self-consciousness or
issues of identity.

The Seghers story has helped me in another important way: to construct a narrative that depicts time in
terms of personal accuracy, one that allows the past to
suddenly slice into a time line that is chronologically
still in the present. Some stories that follow are interrupted by another tense. All are shadowed by sensibilities forged by experiences outside Northern Ireland

that have shaped my representation of memory. The final two stories are about recent experiences in France and Germany, yet they are also, if not equally, shaped by growing up in Northern Ireland.

I build my journey on the ground I know best—the hills around Belfast—not on the County Antrim side of the lough but on the County Down side. This will give us direct access to the roads that will later take us on a holiday to Newcastle and a day's outing to Strangford Lough. We'll dutifully write essays about both excursions. We'll also go way beyond Belfast to France and meet there later on as adults. But first we must try to learn the language. And finally, we'll end up in a Jewish graveyard in Bavaria, long after I have learned to work with the language. Occasionally, I will remember that I am writing this in Wisconsin but just occasionally and then only to situate myself in my most immediate present.

For purposes of orientation I am providing in this introduction a personalized road map out of Belfast by way of one of two main arteries—the Ormeau Road or the posher Malone Road, which were covered in my father's day by tramlines and in my day by the green bus, No. 13, to be exact. Today city buses still cover part of the same route, up to the end of the Malone Road or to the end of the Ormeau Road; the former will leave you within a healthy walking distance of the Mary Peters track, built in honor of our famous Olympic athlete; the latter will drop you off near a large supermarket where women dress up to shop for groceries.

Sadly, the once locally owned shop has been replaced by a big, bossy English import designed to look like an American-style shopping plaza but without American efficiency, which any one of us can live without, but a shop that runs out of wheaten bread (called farls locally) in the middle of the afternoon in Belfast should be closed for health reasons.

If you take the Malone bus, it would be better to go in the spring when the daffodils are in bloom in Barnett's Park, right at the end of the lines. Barnett used to be an actual person, but now his big mansion is operated by the National Trust, which just goes to show that the rest of us will get to roam around big mansions sooner or later. You could walk your dog on the towpath along the River Lagan, but don't look too long into the water, for they say there is a man in there—at least what's left of him—stuffed in a mattress and anchored down with two stones, a casualty of the Troubles. (The towpath was recently closed during the foot-and-mouth scare.) Keep on going all the way up to Edenderry Village, formerly called "The Cage" because of its reputation for entrapping visiting suitors, who quickly found themselves living with the mother-in-law in one of the factory-owned houses until an identical one—down to the very wallflowers in the front garden—became available. A few of the old-timers have survived the demise of the local Irish linen factory, which provided work and wives for many generations. You'll know the old-timers by the pigeon loft in their back garden, but I take back my advice about going in spring, for that's when the pigeons embark on the races that go on throughout the summer, and the least whisper could lose a man a good race and a better bet that he'll win it. Sadly, all the pigeon races were cancelled in the spring of 2001 because of foot-and-mouth disease. Surely, nothing in life is more futile than a pigeon with nowhere to fly. It's as bad as a manuscript without a publisher.

If you take the Ormeau bus, you can get a visual sense of the Catholic-Protestant divide from the safety of your seat. From the bus window you'll see street names at the bottom end of the road—Jerusalem Street, Palestine Street, Damascus Street—that may baffle you (clearly, someone took William Blake's poem very seriously: "And did those feet in ancient time / Walk upon England's mountains green? . . . And was Jerusalem builded here / Among those dark satanic hills?"). But try to imagine that the Gasworks is still going strong, and you'll smell the mincemeat that was served up for our school dinners. If smell can evoke color, then mincemeat is pitch black with an acrid taste. As you travel toward the Lagan River, you'll notice the Irish tricolor waving from windows in the side streets, and you will instantly understand why the authorities are not keen to see the Ballynafeigh Orangemen marching with unfurled British Union Jacks and banners on which King Billy is depicted crossing the Boyne. When you reach the end of the line, there is not

much to see, except for the well-dressed grocery shoppers or the gates of Foster Greene Hospital, where
many in the province died of tuberculosis when I was a
child. Oddly enough, the well-dressed shoppers look
neither Protestant nor Catholic.

My school—the subject of several of these stories—
lay halfway between the Ormeau Road and the Malone
Road, geographically close enough to the Gasworks to
be contaminated by some solidly proletarian odors yet
not close enough to the Malone Road to fall under the
chillingly correct pronunciation of vowels. I have dis-
guised some of the names, just in case any surviving
teacher is not amused by my fictionalized memories.
Miss Crone, of course, remains Miss Crone. This is
a great pity, for some of them had names that corresponded with complete accuracy to their persons.
Adam himself could not have done a better job in nam-
ing the creatures of Eden. The stories I tell, on and
about the teachers, are like all the stories in this book,
more real than true. Family members are another problem. I refuse to divulge the names of my late uncles because in their lifetime they were so shy and reclusive
that they would blush in their graves at the thought of
being mentioned in public. In fact, the younger one
was so shy that he had to write away for white geraniums rather than ask for something so unusual at the
local nursery. As for the others, I have tried to find
names for them that somehow correspond to the
cadence of their real ones.

The stories begin in and move on from school, which is as good a place as any to observe national identity (or its suppression) and certainly not the worst site from which to comment on a country's commitment to the next generation. Because I wasn't good at sums, my school in Belfast prepared me to read literature, even when it was written in foreign languages. Frankly, I am irritated when someone in the United States asks me how in the world I ever came to speak German—as if it were some wildly exotic language and its acquisition in as remote and perilous a place as Northern Ireland (invariably followed by the indescribably boring question, "Do you speak German with an Irish accent?") constituted another wonder of the world. I am not sure whether there was a plot to send people who liked foreign languages away from the province, but in my case it worked, for I went to cities and towns that had no streets like Ormeau Road, not even Jerusalem, though it certainly shares and exceeds the number of bomb alerts.

Yet as far as I wandered beyond Belfast, something deeper always drew me back, even during the height of the Troubles, those years of torture that have dogged the life of every man, woman, and child who lives in Northern Ireland or has fled from it. I personally resented being stared at by police officers on arrival from Belfast at mainland airports, and my American teenagers hated having to do the talking in an English hotel because their mother's accent was enough to set off the suggestion of a bomb in her bag. So I do not drag in the story about the man who did time in the Maze Prison to satisfy the prerequisite for narratives of the north of Ireland. I wrote about him because I have known men like him all my life, the ones who stayed, who became bricklayers or joiners, ducking and diving at odd jobs in their free time, reading the *Racing Gazette.* And now these hard men help me understand both the place I left and the people I left behind. Just don't thank them for being good informants or they'll wince.

The first story is about my father, when he was a lad going to Purdysburn School, the same school I attended for two years. I have kept the school name intact in case anyone wants to have a look at the old schoolhouse, still standing where the Ballycoan Road separates from the road to Ballylesson, on the brow of the hill beyond the Belvoir Hospital, formerly known as Purdysburn Fever Hospital and now apparently under threat of closure. It was built around 1918 with red brick carted from the builders, H. G. Martin's. I know because my father used to tell the story. It is worth repeating.

The horse that was pulling the cart strunted (refused to budge) on its way up the hill, happily just as Sam Harrison was going toward town on what my dad called a truckle cart—a small wooden cart—pulled by a bullock called Bob. Of course, Sam stopped and offered Bob's service to the despairing driver, who turned it down, until Sam bet him ten bob that Bob the Bullock could do the job. Well, Sam and the driver propped up the load of brick with a cog behind the wheel, eased the cart shaft up, and backed Bob into the spot where the horse had stood. He then yoked up Bob, putting the drafts on the bullock's hems. Sam then hopped up on the foreball (the front) of the cart and gave Bob a crack with an eighteen-inch pigskin whip. Sam Harrison won his bet, and the red brick from H. G. Martin's was deposited at the building site. My dad said that Bob's feat was the talk of the townland (township) and possibly the whole county. He never missed the chance for hyperbole.

I return, however, to the main road, for we have now reached Purdysburn corner, in full view of the gray stone elementary school built on a gentle incline. Though the whole province is now serviced by decent roads and a rail service that has functioned fine despite thirty years of bomb scares, modernization has yet to reach the roads around Purdysburn, where the No. 13 bus still has to bully its way up the narrow road to Drumbo, driving halfway up the hedge to let a compact car pass. Like many of the one-room schoolhouses in the United States, Purdysburn School is now inhabited by an actual person and for all I know more than one of them. I would hope that it is no longer heated with a coke-burning pot-bellied stove in the corner of each room.

The leitmotifs of two stories are pigeons and cattle and by association pigeon clubs and cattle marts—two grossly neglected models for the promotion of sectarian harmony. I am amazed that someone has not made a documentary about the pigeon as a symbol of peace in Irish life—and I mean the whole island. You could swoop into one of the Dublin lofts on a Saturday afternoon during an all-Ireland pigeon race and then bring your camera up to the North to observe the very same sense of stillness and reverence that unites these men, who are patiently waiting for their little birds to wing their way back into the loft from as far away as Penzance, Dinard, St. Malo, Nantes, and Reims, through the trap door into the loft. Then the birds are tenderly scooped up by hands callused from manual work. The pigeon racer gently inserts the little ringed leg into the clock that will time the birds' long journey and bring honor to their owner and to their club. Instruct the camera operator to linger for a while on the response to the question I recently asked, "What is so unique about the pigeon?" and the man may answer, "The way it will let a magpie eat out its little heart without a struggle." Or he may tell you what Oliver Gourley said to Kirker Cochrane when Oliver's favorite pigeon, which he had named "Wee Albert," failed to return from the Dinard race. "You lost a great pigeon," said Kirker by way of condolence. "No," replied Oliver, "I lost a great friend." Wee Albert was a mealy cock, a pinkish color with two red bars, and for three years he *cleaned up* the club, winning prize after prize each Saturday—until the day he didn't turn up from France. He should be the star of the film. In the documentary you will also learn that fret marks become etched on the bird after a long-distance race and that it typically loses as much as two-thirds of its weight. But it keeps on flying, for love of its partner and its loft are stronger forces than the north winds that impede it on its way home.

Yet I very much doubt that the story of Wee Albert ever made it into the briefings on Northern Ireland given during presidential visits, like President Bill Clinton's in 1995. And I doubt that he would have known to ask what a perfect pigeon looked like or understood the answer: "pear shaped and tapering away." Did anyone ever suggest that Clinton visit a cattle mart instead of invoking fictional Irish ancestors on the most politicized turf in the province? He could have been photographed leaning on the railings at Saintfield or Enniskillen cattle mart, chatting away with Catholic and Protestant farmers on either side of him, in a stunning visual representation of solidarity, everyone united in a common love and respect for cattle. It would have done wonders for his image and released a refreshingly different picture of the province to the world. And afterward in the back cafe he could have had an Ulster fry swimming in lard with all the trimmings: fried bread—potato or wheat—thickly cut slices of bacon, fried egg, fried tomato, mushrooms, and perhaps a lamb chop and a slice of liver. Clinton would be a grand advertisement for the local dish.

I suppose I could still excise the last two stories about France and Germany and give the manuscript a nice, simple, finished look, which might improve textual aesthetics and promote a better chance to be noticed in the market for Irishness. But they are my personal connection to histories and cultures that have challenged my own "either green or orange" identity model and provided colors for my text that I had to discover for myself.

Besides, thousands of us living beyond Belfast are still connected to it, we whose ears are cocked for the unmistakable sounds of our native tongue. Like the woman who served our table in a restaurant in Munich. She said she spoke English after she heard us discussing the menu, and right away I heard in her response the North Irish vowels. This Antrim-born woman moved in and out of European languages as effortlessly and elegantly as she moved across the restaurant that she owned with her Italian husband, turning one moment to address him in Italian, chiding her children in English as they were helping their parents, and serving the tables outside in the bright sunshine, speaking in flawless German that had just a trace of a Bavarian accent.

"That was great *craic*" were the parting words of a woman clearly glad to connect, if briefly, with someone from home. It's the lure of good *craic* that draws us into conversations like this with Irish people from every county in the whole island, no matter where we are in the world. But it's the particular impact of North Irish consonants clanging around among loosely held vowels that evokes an immediate bridge, an audible if intangible madeleine that invites us to come back to the six counties.

In my first week at Trinity College, Dublin, a student with a terminally English accent from Derry (she always called it Londonderry) told me that if I wanted to be accepted at Trinity, I would have to lose my North Irish accent. She called it dreadful. (I wonder what on earth became of her?) Not that my accent and speech habits don't grate on my own nerves, especially when I get excited and repeat a point. I do. So I do. (That's the main reason the peace talks took so long.) And yet the old vernacular can be a life saver. Here in Wisconsin I once knew a man from Northern Ireland who asked me to talk about home. He was on his deathbed. All he wanted was to hear sounds of home. And I provided them. And then he died.

"What a *dreech* [dreary] place to lie" was how his nephew from County Down later described his uncle's burial ground. He had just visited the gravesite in a large cemetery in Waukesha County. I told him about the litany of names I pronounced at his uncle's bedside, starting in Ballynahinch, working my way along the main road to Newcastle, pausing to mention by name every market town I could remember, to refresh the soul of a man who was dying far away from the farm he had left more than forty years earlier.

The Jewish graveyard at the end of this collection of stories was one of the least *dreech* places I have ever visited, but unlike the big, plain, open cemetery in

Waukesha, the brutally interrupted history of the Jewish cemetery belies the peace and beauty of the surroundings. So this little graveyard in Bavaria has the last word, alongside stories of Northern Ireland. May it rest in peace. In the eighties Seamus Heaney once wrote to the *Irish Times:* "Poetry is defined by its energies and its eloquence, not by the passport of the poet or the editor; or the name of the nationality. That way lie all the categories, the separations, the censorships that poetry exists to dispel." These stories are not poetry, but they seek to point in the direction of people and places that dispel the kinds of separations that our history has imposed upon us or that we have imposed upon ourselves.

Acknowledgments

I want to express my gratitude to Isobel and Alfred Bader, who have been an enormous source of encouragement to me in the course of writing these stories. Among my colleagues at the University of Wisconsin–Milwaukee, I wish to thank Rachel Baum, Michael Fountain, and Richard Monti, who read the first draft. Robert Stern of the University of Massachusetts also provided helpful advice. Without their encouragement I might never have gone on. I am deeply grateful to Michael Gillespie of Marquette University and Eammon Wall of the University of St. Louis, who provided valuable insights for the final draft. Special thanks to my husband and children and to the friends who have patiently listened to or read these stories over the years, among them, John Duckhorn, Lilian McCann, and Alice Tate.

I

The Wee Wild One

In 1916, two years into the Great War, my father walked out of school after throwing an ink pot at his teacher, Harry MacIntosh. My father's parting words were, "Come on, Mamie, we're going home," addressed as much to the stunned pupils as to his little sister, whose severe learning disability had just provoked MacIntosh to poke her so hard in the ribs that she had burst into tears. Her big brother—the Wee Wild One, as by now he was known—had instantly jumped to her defense with the nearest weapon he could find, thus ending his education at Purdysburn School (where his own son would get into a different kind of trouble right after the Second World War). From the day he threw the inkpot, my dad and Mamie would make their way each morning up the lane that skirted the Stable Brae, past Rob Cammock's thatched cottage, past the Wilgars's farm, to the road that would lead them to their new school in Drumbo. Mamie never finished her schooling and died in her early teens of diabetes—in those days incurable. The Wee Wild One had to steady himself on the stair railings, so great was his grief when they sang "Safe in the Arms of Jesus" just before her little coffin was carried out of the house.

3

Though only a couple of miles away, Drumbo was in alien territory, producing people whose collective character was as different to people reared in Ballycoan as the ideological differences that now separate North and South Korea. Still, Drumbo School was better by far than the one in Purdysburn, what with Harry MacIntosh's liking for the older girls, two of whom he openly fondled on his knee—the one that was not wooden. He did all his teaching around the open fire, resulting in a permanently singed trouser leg—the one that was wooden. In fact, he sat so close to the fire one day that he set the leg alight, and a pupil (not my father, who looked the other way) had to douse it with a bucket of water. Mr. Bates, the Drumbo teacher, was a different man altogether, which became apparent the first time the Wee Wild One got into a fight at the bottom of Ballycairn Hill, where he squared off against a boy twice his size for taunting Tishy Martin that she attended a mission hall and not a real church (Tishy held my dad's schoolbag and cheered him on). The incident quickly reached the ears of Mr. Bates, who allowed his pugnacious pupil to leave school five minutes early the next day to avoid another fight. Mr. Bates needn't have bothered, for the Wee Wild One waited behind the hedge and surprised the older boy with a hiding that resulted in a consultation with the Wee Wild One's mother, whose wet dishcloth subsequently proved to be more effective than all the wisdom of the teacher. Still, it was worth it, just to stand up to one of those big

Drumbo bullies that was reared on oul whins (old gorse) and had no call at all to be so conceited.

In the years that led up to the province's becoming Northern Ireland (of course, some would say it was gerrymandered), the education of the Wee Wild One played out against a backdrop of virulent hostility toward anyone who opposed Unionism, which was expressed in songs like "Slooter slaughter, holy boiling water / We'll scatter the papishes everywhere," to quote one example of the verbal sophistication that shaped schoolchildren of the 1920s. And all this occurred in the intense atmosphere of big drums, bands, and marches. This was intoxicating stuff, and the Wee Wild One was not beneath following a band, no matter where it was going to or coming from, like the evening he followed the big drums all the way to Drumbo, after Sir William Craig, an early Unionist known for his fiery speeches, had addressed a political rally at Blakeley's farm. The only problem was that the Wee Wild One's mother was unimpressed when he finally appeared barefoot at the door and politicized him into a different kind of home rule with the wet dishcloth.

But other forms of education were readily available in rural Northern Ireland. In my father's case it was Sam Harrison, the man who had named him the Wee Wild One. A distant relative and a dropout from Trinity College, Dublin, Sam had arrived at the door one day and announced to my grandmother, "I'm back home to stay." And he did, dying many years later in the little two-room stone cottage up the lane from our house. But that will come later. Sons reared on the land in Northern Ireland received their fair share of education from the men who worked alongside them, often laborers from the bordering counties of the Republic who had been drawn north to earn a living, which amounted to their keep, two ounces of tobacco, and eighteen bob a week. And if he was a powerful good eater like Jimmy Craney, his keep was a significant expense for his employer. Jimmy had come from Monaghan to work on a neighboring farm, hired to face hedges and clean sheughs (ditches). He finally got so fed up with the daily diet of herring that he threw down his tools and threatened to leave. When asked where he would go, Jimmy replied, "I'm going up the river to spawn."

But Sam was in a different category, not only because he was related but because his kind heart and gentle ways had endeared him to the youngest son of the family to which he was indentured. Sam loved his whiskey and his pipe, the former so much that he had to leave Trinity, but the experience had sobered him enough to fulfill his farm duties, and he never touched whiskey on the job. The pipe was another matter, and that's where the Wee Wild One came in handy, for his hands were smaller than Sam's, and my father could fairly rub the tobacco fine and put it into the clay pipe, standing back to see if it was drawing free or not. He had mastered the technique to perfection yet without ever taking up smoking himself, which says more about Sam than his charge. From Sam the Wee Wild One learned how to get along with horses (and Bob the bullock), how to know their every mood and whim. The horse was a family member, not some creature to ride or bully along in a field. Horses had names that gave them the dignity that they deserved—not frivolous Pony Club names like Bubbles or Cackles. The two horses that completed our family were called Ned and Dolly. They also had family names that further reflected the respect in which they were held. Ned's full name was Ned Horse and Dolly's was Dolly Mare. If there were such a thing as a Horse Register, that's exactly how their lives would be documented. (You would simply look under the years 1915–30 under *H* and *M,* and you would find both.)

As family members, Ned Horse and Dolly Mare were not beneath being drawn into coarse, frankly vulgar, behavior. This became painfully apparent each time the Harrison sisters came to visit, and one horse was as bad as the other. The Wee Wild One was sent to meet the tram at the end of the Malone Road with one of the two horses strapped to as fine a trap as money could buy. The sisters, cousins of my grandmother, were both single women of a certain age, highly educated and polished. In fact, they were so polished that they chose to travel by Malone Road, rather than face the possibility of contamination along the shorter Ormeau Road route. They lived in Bangor along the sea front and did not say aye for yes or *fornent* for "in front of." Their little finger was a social weapon, held at a firm right angle when they drank their tea later in the parlor with my grandmother. But first they had to get there, and that's where the Wee Wild One came in—in collusion, of course, with Dolly Mare or Ned Horse— each thinking that he or she was in control.

As soon as the two finely dressed women were set- tled into the trap, off they set down the hill toward the River Lagan, over Shaw's Bridge (where the mattress is supposed to be), through Milltown Village, and headed to the right toward home, Ash Hill, as our house was called. The hill *fornent* Purdysburn Fever Hospital— where Bob Bullock distinguished himself—was their first obstacle, and that's where horse power kicked in. The Wee Wild One knew how to tap Dolly or Ned's belly just at the right spot so that it looked like he was encouraging the horse up the hill. Neither horse ever let him down. Nor did the women let themselves or their class down. When Dolly Mare or Ned Horse let off wind, just as they were passing the front gates of the Fever Hospital, the Harrison sisters did not blink. And when they made their return trip in the trap after their monthly visit, the older one carefully took a sixpence piece from her little satin bag and handed it to my father with the words, "Here is a little piece of silver. Don't spend it on ciggies."

Another educator, not a person but a ubiquitous presence of the twenties, was emigration, especially to the United States. (The twenties would become an even more pervasive decade after a series of wet springs blighted the potato harvest so seriously that farmers thought they were about to face the kind of famine that had decimated the island in the previous century.) Almost every farming family has a story of the brother, in our case three, who said his goodbye to grieving parents. The farewell was right at the front door. There were no promises of return, no assurances they would phone on arrival, no e-mail addresses, no fax numbers to span the miles. My eldest uncle, an engineer by trade, had emigrated earlier from Ballycoan to Seattle and soon found himself in an American uniform in Le Havre, discharging ammunition from a warship. Without the Great War, Uncle Archie would not have been able to visit Ash Hill for a whole week during the war. His little brother—young enough to have been his child—was raised with stories about the tears that were shed when the time came to get into the trap. Archie's own and only son would be shot down over Belgium in the last weeks of World War II, also in an American uniform. His grave is in the Ardennes. My dad told me when I was a child about the American cousin who had died in the war. I cried when the man in charge of the graveyard gave me my cousin's serial number. That was in 1997.

There are no tears, however, in the story about Gordie Taylor, though he too was leaving the province for good. The Wee Wild One was helping Sam Harrison shore a drain (ensure proper drainage) in a five-acre field when Gordie arrived with a gun in his hand. He had bought it for eight quid in Hunter's Gun Shop on Royal Avenue, and now he was heading for the United States, a country where he thought guns had—at least at this stage—no place. Sam had put down his tools and, to the amazement of the boy at his side, announced, "I want to buy it for the wee one here. I'll give you three pounds and ten shillings." And that from a man who was so afraid of ending up in the poorhouse that he gave my grandmother three shillings a week to save for him.

In fact, the relentless struggle to eke out a living was what made all partings bearable in the end. Surely, America had to offer more than this. And you were treated fairly there, regardless of where you came from, not like here, where there was such injustice. My father's generation was still singing about Gladstone (the pre-revisionist version), even though he had been dead since 1898: "Gladstone's into Parliament and sits among the gents. / He'll let them see how Hill and Ford and Irwin raised the rents." Yet they were still paying rents to the likes of Irwin in the twenties, and would continue to do so for several decades in some parts of the province, unless one of these absentee landlords took a fancy to a daughter (or even a wife) when he made his rounds on horseback to view the land. Nothing lowered the rent on land like offering up a woman. Gladstone would rise in his grave (or maybe not) if he had known.

If you want to confirm the Wee Wild One's stories, just talk to a seventy-five-year-old farmer about growing up on the land near Belfast in the twenties and thirties—someone like John McDowell. He can remember nothing. "There was an *oul* map on the wall" is as far as he will go in geography class. But talk to him about what he learned outside school, and you'll hear the same kind of stories about the land and the people who worked it, the connections to Belfast— going to the market to sell cattle in Allam's cattle mart, getting your lunch in the ITL Cafe—"and *quare* grub it was." And like his lifelong friend, my father, John will also speak of an even greater struggle—the plight of the urban poor. Compassion that has been distilled for more than fifty years has a distinct bouquet. The description of one man pushing his bike up the Cregagh Road in Belfast late one evening is just that—as bland as milk—until you hear John's voice telling it the way it really was. "Thon crittur was that tired he could hardly push the oul bike up the hill. And him wrought the whole day breek-laying and then from six to ten at night in oul toffs' gardens so he could feed the weans [wee ones]." Or ask him how the Catholic workers from Cavan were treated on his farm. And he'll say, "Sure, didn't we let them take the motorcar down to mass in the chapel on the Ormeau Road?"

But John's stories must wait for another day, for it is time for Sam Harrison to die. His badger-skin trousers have been laid aside. The thick black curls are now snow white, his pale face sunken under the long beard. The Wee Wild One has meanwhile become the Boss

and has honored Sam's wish to die where he belonged—
in the cottage that belonged to the farm, his home for
years. It is the dead of winter, and it looks like Sam will
not survive the night. As a gesture of respect for Sam's
Anglican background, my father had driven down to
Ballylesson to alert the minister of the Church of Ireland that Sam was sinking fast. The minister had come
reluctantly, knowing that my father had about as much
enthusiasm for organized religion as Sam himself. But
unlike Sam, the minister was not cynical about faith in
Christ. More than anything, my father was broken-
hearted that he was losing a lifelong friend, without
any promise of meeting him in heaven. Maybe Sam
would at least listen to what the minister had to say, a
verse of hope and comfort from the Gospels. The reverend was barely halfway through the catechism when
Sam looked up from the depths of the bedclothes, eyes
bright as beads, and uttered his last words on earth:
"Sir, let your sermon be as short as possible." "A hardened little wretch," the vicar said as he left the cottage.
But my father did not answer him.

2

"All in the April Evening"

It was supposedly one mile from our house to Purdysburn Elementary School, but apparently this mile did not include the mile-long lane to the main road nor the steep brae on the Ballycoan side of Anna Blakeley's farm, where the Wee Wild One had heard Sir James Craig speak. The most pleasant part of the alleged mile-long walk was picking up the neighbor children en route, as good-natured a bunch of humans as anyone could wish to travel with. Not many families lived on the Ballycoan Road, but those who did had large broods of loud fun-loving children. One family had one daughter and six sons, huge lads who played in the local flute bands—regular Jimmy Galways—always hooting and tooting "Dolly's Brae" or "The Sash" on their flutes—and could be seen walking in Ballylesson Flute Band on the Twelfth of July, their marching shoes polished up for the big commemoration of the Battle of the Boyne. One son was to distinguish himself later by winning first prize at the picnic in Milltown in celebration of the coronation of Her Royal Highness, Queen Elizabeth the Second. This young man was dressed as a mouse, the tail for which costume had been donated by a local to leave. Nobody "graduated" from school. You "left" school, and fourteen was not a year too soon. That's the way it was.

The Ballycoan children more or less timed it so that, as we emerged from our lane, they were coming 'round Connery's Corner, along with five girls from a farm up the road and other stragglers from the Mill Road. I have no recollection of anyone talking, but I know there was a lot of chasing up and down the hedges and some interesting name calling, especially directed at one girl who had a permanent head cold, never used a handkerchief, and instead chose to drag the entire contents of her head up and down with hair-splitting proximity to her upper lip, to be miraculously retrieved at the last second. Hughie Moffat told her that she would be arrested—"for selling candles without wicks." I had no idea then what he meant and, frankly, had little to crow about myself, considering my own mother had to sew buttons on my cuffs to circumvent a shortcut to the handkerchief in my pocket.

One group of children, four boys and one sister who joined us at the bottom of the hill beyond our lane, were very poor. Their father was on the dole and was said to be a socialist. Apparently, he believed that everybody was equal. I could never forget them because our mother held them over our heads as a model of correct attitude, not unlike the way American children are bludgeoned into gratitude with reminders of the starving children of countries that few of their parents could find on a map. My mother would invite these children for tea, and their beautiful table manners put us to shame while we ate stolidly on. Their parting words were always, "Thank you for your kindness and hospitality," which invariably drew another sigh of admiration and compassion from our mother. She was very impressionable.

I spent only two years at Purdysburn School, waiting it out until my legs were long enough to board the No. 13 bus and head for school in Belfast. During those years I learned that lace was made in Nottingham and that the Donegal Mountains were not in Wicklow but Donegal. I know that only because one of the Mulholland boys got the wrong answer and was publicly ridiculed for relocating the mountains. I also met Martha Trumbles. "Pitter-patter went the rain and Martha Trumbles grew wetter and wetter" were the lines that introduced me to literature. No Spot was encouraged to run in the two-room schoolhouse in Purdysburn. Nor was any student ever invited to see Spot run. We lived on a higher literary plane than a dog show, complete with a picture of poor old Martha Trumbles pushing a wheelbarrow up a hill through pelting rain. No wonder the soul grew wetter and wetter.

Beyond the trials of Martha Trumbles and Nottingham lace, I have no recollection of what I learned at Purdysburn nor of the teacher who taught what I can't remember on our side of the two-room school, but I vividly remember the teacher who did not teach me, at least her boots. She was the principal, referred to simply as "Oul Fuzzy," a name she did not deserve for she had a young-looking, attractive face that was framed by pure white hair. Rumor had it that an Englishman had jilted her and her hair turned white, which I tended to believe because I understood the word *jilt* from the photo of a great-aunt on our dining-room wall. She had also been jilted—again by an Englishman, an officer in the British army. So it made sense. What remains in my memory, however, is not the look of a jilted woman but of her boots, which are so dominant that they trample on almost every other memory of the school, except the one about the turnip seeds or "All in the April evening"—but those will come later. An object of amazement, these boots never aged; their beautiful shiny brown leather and snow white fur, which peeped through at the top, looked like new every day. And in my memory she wears them every single day all year, getting off the No. 13 bus at Purdysburn corner in the morning, boarding the bus again at the end of the school day. Always wearing these same boots, rain or shine.

Certain auras, a certain damp atmosphere, linger over the school, perhaps not strong enough to qualify as an out-and-out memory like a wheelbarrow or boots but worth mentioning because they evoke a peacefulness that is rarely associated with a school. The most dominant one is of Billy Lowry, who was cutting corn in the field behind the school, in full view of the outside dry toilet with the pervasive smell of lime. As small as I was, I could see over the door, out into the fields beyond the school, and was already smart enough to know that watching Billy Lowry reap his corn on a

September day was infinitely more pleasant that doing sums indoors, even if getting to watch him entailed having to ask the teacher for a piece of the paper that had been stacked in a neat pile of pages trimmed from the *Belfast Telegraph*. Because everybody, including the two teachers, was in the same boat, no one was embarrassed about walking out the back door of the school with a piece of paper in his or her hand. I certainly could not have been accused of lingering over the news for, after all, I could read only "pitter-patter went the rain and Martha Trumbles grew wetter and wetter."

Then there is the aura of friendliness that verges on a memory, of the Purdysburn Mental Hospital patients leaning over the wall in front of the school. The walled grounds of the hospital—formerly the estate of Lord Batt—extended as far as Purdysburn corner where Oul Fuzzy got off and on the No. 13 bus. The patients loved to lean on the wall, smoke their pipes or cigarettes, and chat with the schoolchildren coming and going to school. The "leavers"—those who were fourteen and were already grown-ups—were known to enjoy the company of the Purdysburn patients, especially if they were able to get a quick drag on a Woodbine. Many years later, in front of the tobacconist's—known locally as "the wee shop," a popular haunt for the Purdysburn patients—a man approached our car, greeted my father through the open window, and asked if I were his daughter. Satisfied with the declaration of paternity, he gave me a compliment to which I cling when my

American dentist treats my North Irish tooth fillings like a dinosaur exhibit: "Sure, and she has lovely teeth."

And then there was the atmosphere of Purdysburn Village. In those days the travelers—they were called gypsies then—used to park their caravan at the end of the village. It is now a village for the elderly and actually has won prizes for being one of the best kept in the province. (I am thinking of getting on the waiting list.) It is always a Mediterranean summer when I think of the village, always unrealistically warm, and there are always overly elderly people sitting on the bench, all smoking pipes, watching us children every week on our way to Sunday school in the little hall at the bottom of the village. There was a burn (stream) at the bottom of the hill where we spotted trout, and on the other side of the wall the same row of men from the Mental—as it was called—engaging us in a chat. I still see one boy the same age as I; he was called Jackie, and he was dark haired and wiry. He was to die along with three others at the height of the Troubles in the Stag, a pub less than two miles away, as he was having a pint with his mates. But in my memory his head has not been shot off, and he is leaning forward to receive a sweet from the teacher, Bobby Lowry, for saying his verses. Or Jackie is chasing up and down the village, racing past the elderly people who are all smoking pipes.

Another vivid memory of Purdysburn School comes secondhand but from a very reliable source. There was the day that Oul Fuzzy decided to beautify the front lawn of the school and asked the children in early spring to bring along seeds that they would plant. A city woman, she was all excited about things like seeds, which most of the schoolchildren took for granted, especially as many of them returned home after school to *sned* (cut the ends off) turnips, plant potatoes, and spend most of their free time straddling tractors up and down steep hills. And now Oul Fuzzy wanted them to plant seeds in the flower beds in front of the school and was acting like it was a great adventure. How delightful it would be, she rhapsodized, to watch the tender growth of the little seedlings and see them pop through the soil in late spring. Not all had caught the excitement; among those who were less than excited was my brother, who arrived at school with a brown bag full of turnip seeds, which Oul Fuzzy did not identify as such, and gratefully received, along with all the other seeds that would later emerge as bona fide flowers, like sweet pea and daisies. She was not amused when my brother's "wallflowers" turned out to be turnips yet was too indebted to my brother for delivering her fresh eggs every week to give him a hiding. His simple explanation was that it was funny how you could be mistaken. She was ripping.

"All in the April Evening," however, is no aura. It is a memory. Even though it sounds all wispy and spring-like, especially when you hear the next line—"April airs were abroad. The sheep with their lambs / Passed me by on the road,"—it is—at least to me—as hard as the

21

Ballymagarrick blue slate on the roof of Ballylesson Church. And it becomes even more wispy and haunting because the last line is repeated—"The sheep with their lambs / Passed me by on the road." The thing is, it might not come over as particularly haunting in cold print like this, but it was actually sung, and the "lambs" of the last line were emphasized like they were "lamb-ambs," giving a very strong pastoral resonance. This was the song—or hymn, if you insist—that the children practiced for weeks before the final performance during Easter week at Ballylesson Church of Ireland. Presbyterians were included with the Anglicans, for at least they had been christened. The trouble was that some of us did not fit into the ecclesiastical scheme of things. The vicar from the Church of Ireland and the Presbyterian minister came in weekly to catechize—or "christianize"—the others, unwittingly providing some powerful arguments for the separation of church and state. These clergy were treated with extraordinary reverence, especially the Anglican vicar, who had been educated at Trinity College, Dublin, and was called "highly educated." There was, of course, the implication that the Presbyterian minister was not in the vicar's league, so presumably was "lowly educated." But some of us were in a different league altogether. Not that we were ignorant. We had learned Psalm 103 by heart at Sunday School: "Bless the Lord, O my soul, and all that is within me. Bless His Holy name. Bless the Lord, O my soul, and forget not all His benefits."

And we knew John 3:16—the Old King James version: "For God so loved the world that He gave His only begotten Son, that whosoever believeth in Him should not perish but hath everlasting life." Maybe we did not yet understand the Gospels, but we sang with reckless abandon on many a Sunday down the village "When mothers of Salem their children brought to Jesus / The stern disciples drove them back / And bade them depart. / But Jesus saw them where they were / And sweetly looked and kindly said / 'Suffer the little children to come unto me.'" But for now, some kind of action had to be taken toward children who did not belong. So against the strains of the Irish poet Katharine Tynan's "All in the April Evening," we were sent outside to play—with the gypsy children—little travelers who were delighted to chase around the schoolyard with the other children of Salem.

3
The Actual Building

Princess Gardens School was located at the bottom end of University Street, within shouting distance of Botanic Avenue, which could have been corroborated by passers-by when Miss Smith was teaching algebra. "What a little ninny," she would rant when one of us could not make x + y equal what she wanted it to equal. "A silly little ninny" was her final judgment. The school was actually a house and had every right to look like a house, for that's precisely what it had been in the mid-1800s, when patricians chose to live on streets rather than avenues, upper avenues, closes, lanes, and gardens. Admittedly, the trend has not descended into the name calling found in many of the modern subdivisions, which seem to have either bucolic sounding names like Misty Meadows or Anglo-Saxon ones like Gloucester Ridge.

Princess Gardens was located on a block that consisted of several solidly built three-story terrace houses that apparently were considered suitable for schools, as there was another school—a secretarial one—a few doors away. Princess Gardens was actually comprised of two houses, connected at the second story by a long corridor that housed the school office and the first form's room. But few, if any, pupils ever thought of

Princess Gardens as a house—maybe a barracks but certainly not a house. The name of the school was discreetly engraved on a brass sign on the low wall that set the parameters of the school. Steps led to the heavy front door, the one used by everybody except the headmistress, who swept in the other equally heavy door to the left, dramatically late every day. Two large rooms opened off the main foyer in each building, one for the second form and the other, on the right, for the staff. The school gymnasium and the headmistress's office were on the other side, which explains why the headmistress used that door, if not why she was always late.

The staff room doubled as a lunchroom but bore little or no resemblance to a room for humans, least of all teachers, to eat in or even sit in. During their occasional free period we could see the teachers slumped over books at four tables with eight backless benches. Gas fires, the only means of heating the entire school (with the exception of the headmistress's office), spluttered gently behind the teachers, the sole recipients of their warmth. We girls shivered in the three rows of desks lined up in front of the teacher's desk and instantly descended on the fire the minute she left the room. Occasionally, we were allowed to open the windows, though this was rare because the high ceilings took care of ventilation. I have some memory of June days warm enough to allow fresh air in the room. I mention this deliberately, as the opening of a window was a happening. A long pole that looked like a grappling hook was carefully inserted in a little knob at the top of the window and then pulled downward. A teacher would instruct a mature pupil, who also was of average or above-average height, to open the window. The rest of us would observe, secretly wishing that we were taller and more mature. "Silly ninnies" were never asked to open the window.

Tucked in at the back of the ground floor was the kitchen. Here Mrs. Wilson turned out the school dinner, for which we queued in orderly fashion (a much-used expression) in the middle of the day. Supervised by bossy prefects, we wound our way down one of the two stairways to the rooms that doubled as lunch-rooms. (There was a lot of doubling in the school.) Large trays of steaming food had been handed out through a window from the kitchen to three teachers, who wore an apron, a maternal touch that fooled none of the girls. The teachers recited the same prayer daily: "For what we are about to receive, may the Lord make us truly thankful. Amen." It was a work of deep grace to muster up a crumb of gratitude for the mincemeat that always smelled to me—as I have already pointed out—of the Gas Works on the Ormeau Road, but the Bakewell tart was a credit to the kitchen.

Lists that established the seating arrangements were read out in assembly at the beginning of each school term—a death sentence, if you ended up at a table where a teacher pried into your family life, your father's profession (or lack thereof), or your denominational affiliation. We were all Protestants (with the exception of one Jewish girl, whom we claimed as one of us because she was not Catholic), so the prying for a denomination was not sectarian but simply to ferret out low church girls or possibly girls from two-up-two-down houses on streets like Albion Street off Great Victoria Street.

Prefects were sometimes chosen to head the table, based mostly on obsequiousness toward the senior mistress the year before. A clean plate policy, an unwritten by-law of the school's constitution, was enforced rigorously. The art of spitting a piece of tough beef (we always blamed tough beef on Argentina, probably because we didn't know where it was) into one's napkin was practiced with varying degrees of success. Nothing could be left on the plate, unless you had a note from home, and even then the reason had to be an ulcer, preferably of the bleeding variety. Each day a prefect went from table to table with a pencil and paper at the ready, in case a girl was found without a table napkin, a major infraction, which resulted in a twopence fine. The trick, of course, was never to bring the napkin home, and the result was a health hazard, as more and more food was rescued from digestion. It was entirely reasonable to accumulate a butcher's shop in a table napkin by the end of one school year.

The second floor of the school housed five classrooms, the cloakrooms, the music room, and the corridor, which had been renovated to hold the school office.

The cloakrooms were the equivalent of the locker room in a U.S. high school but without lock and key, and certainly without the possessions that are typically found in American lockers, some of which could be rented out to an average-size family. The idea that anyone would steal from you was absurd, not because of moral considerations but because nothing you had was worth taking, for everything you owned looked exactly the same and just as dull as the next person's. In short, there was no incentive to steal. You kept your "locker" possessions in a cloth bag hung on the knob assigned to you—gym shoes and street or house shoes, depending on whether you were coming or going. There was not a single carpet in the whole building, which resulted in a low if constant noise of feet clumping around on the bare wooden floors. Two secretaries ruled the office and appeared occasionally to remind us that there were other forms of life beyond teachers. One played the organ so acceptably that she was treated as an equal by some teachers, and she was even invited to accompany the hymn on Speech Day. Because of the physical limitations of the school, all major events, like the Christmas play and Speech Day, had to be held in other venues, which meant that parents never had any reason to come to the school and were thus fundamentally separated from the daily life of a child. Yet because the school play and Speech Day were major events in school life, I shall mention them briefly, even though they did not take place in the actual building. I simply

want to pay homage to my favorite teacher, Miss
Orton. The first lines I said on stage at the annual play
were "I am a poor country mouse, and I feel quite
afraid in this rich man's house." Miss Orton stood
prompting in the wings while we mice scampered on
and off the stage, in front of an audience that included
my mother, who looked so proud of her little mouse
that I nearly forgot my lines. We quickly progressed to
Shakespeare and a production of *A Midsummer Night's
Dream,* with props that the average broom closet could
match. But Miss Orton was never at a loss when it
came to imagination and creativity, and she produced a
play that would be the envy of the American Players, the
rep company in Spring Green, Wisconsin. We practiced
in the gym, where Miss Orton's sense for the theatri-
cal and delight in language transformed many a "silly
ninny" into a grand wee actress.

Speech Day, however, was an even bigger event.
In fact, it was an outing, since we had to walk "in orderly fashion" all the way down Botanic Avenue to the
Wellington Hall in downtown Belfast. It was the only
day in the year when every girl in the school wore a
starched blouse and spotless uniform. Although Speech
Day did, as the name implies, include speeches, it was
the day you received your prize for the accumulation of
*A*s and *A*–s—all watched by your parents, who sat in
the galleries above. Prize winners walked solemnly
across the platform, shook the hand of the dignitary
(gloved if a woman), and returned with equal poise to

the seats assigned to the clever and gifted. The prizes were barely worth carrying home—or so we thought then—with titles like *The Observer's Book of British Wildflowers* (my first form prize "for good work in music"). Curiously, it survived the cynicism and now humbly occupies a lower shelf in my library.

On Speech Day teachers wore the hoods with their academic gowns over smart clothes that we had never seen all year. Queens University, Belfast, was the most prominently represented, with Trinity College, Dublin, the runner-up. The whole school sang a hymn that we had been practicing for the last month—usually a rousing one like "Glorious Things of Thee Are Spoken" or "Praise God from Whom All Blessings Flow." One year I had to accompany the hymn "And Did Those Feet in Ancient Times?" which scared me off Blake and a musical score with five flats for life. The school choir sang a song that had involved after-school practice and a late bus home. Even a merry song like "By Dimpled Brook and Fountain Stream" became a real drag, despite the presence of wood nymphs and fairies dancing all over the place.

The Headmistress's Report was supposedly the centerpiece of the event and in fact was actually printed in mercifully abbreviated form the next day in the *Belfast Telegraph*—of course, without the opening lines, "Mister Chairman, Your Grace, Governors of Princess Gardens, Ladies, Gentlemen and Girls." The bulk of the speech celebrated the lives of retiring teachers and bore little or no resemblance to classroom performance, while the rest focused on declining funding from the government. The visiting dignitary's little speech was just as hyperbolic, for it inevitably alluded to what a splendid bunch we girls and all the teachers were.

Speech Day was far removed in time and space from the rest of the school year, and it was hard to return the next day to the same routine, minus the practice for school choir. Nothing had changed. Occasionally, a decent story in English class, like Hardy's *The Woodlanders* would transform the dreary rooms, their walls painted an institutional green that closed in on our imagination. It was hard going after we had graduated from the lower forms, where at least they admitted those wonderful winged horses from Greece and fairies straight from our very own soil. All these years later I can still quote from "The Faeries":

> Up the airy mountain,
> Down the rushy glen,
> We daren't go a-hunting
> For fear of little men;
> Wee folk, good folk,
> Trooping all together;
> Green jacket, red cap,
> And white owl's feather!

The classrooms that housed the third and fourth forms on the second floor were a bit lively, for at least they had a view. Two faced University Street and provided excellent entertainment at lunchtime, when by dint of peeping on tip toes over the top of the half-curtained section of the window, we could observe street life. Every living creature that made its way along University Street in that half-hour fell under our scrutiny, from the wonderfully colorful woman with blond hair on an aging head to the boarders who came and went in the corner house. The blonde woman turned up as a famous sculptor in the *Belfast Telegraph* one day, a discovery that was duly reported to us by another voyeur, generating an even livelier interest in the daily sighting.

The cheapest and arguably lowest form of our window activities was the prurient interest we took in the cars, or should I say "car," that the teachers drove. Maybe there is not, in fact, anything inherently funny about a Morris Minor, but the very sight of that hapless vehicle had the effect of reducing us to helpless laughter. (And to think it is now a status symbol in the United States.) With one exception, the teachers who could afford a car drove a Morris Minor, and they offered a daily diversion, especially if a teacher had gone out at lunchtime and was attempting to park. The half curtain billowed then with our hysterical laughter as we dissolved behind its shelter.

Several girls lived close enough to go home for lunch, and one in particular gave us something to live for. This sixteen-year-old, already an attractive young woman, had a boyfriend with a dashing little red Triumph sports car who dropped her off outside the school. Although the sight underscored the drab existence of the rest of us, it gave us a working model of the opposite of a teacher attempting to park a Morris Minor and introduced us to a life beyond University Street. Maybe we didn't have to settle for a Morris Minor. There could be other cars in the world, and they might drop one of us off in full view of the school. And we would refuse to get out.

There were three main toilets in the whole school. These were used only at break time, and even then it was not openly encouraged, which could explain the major plumbing problems that some of us have suffered in our post–Princess Gardens life. In the ten years I spent at the school, no teacher ever was seen either coming from or going to the bathroom. The closest I ever came to seeing a teacher with human needs was the day I discovered the history teacher in the staff room with her shoes off.

The gym was the original drawing room of the house and was huge, at least the memory of it. The only equipment that we used was an ancient vaulting horse that Miss Warren dragged out for us to jump over. She stood at the ready in case any of us would trip, but considering that it was only about three feet tall, even the chubbiest among us was able to drag over the horse. Bars had been erected along the walls, and from these we hung, stripped down to a blouse and our baggy brown knickers. When the longer days of spring came, we walked up to the playing fields on Ormeau Road—the one shunned by the Harrison sisters but not by Hillary Clinton, who in 1994 was to sit down with Protestant and Catholic women, probably glad to forget her own troubles over a good cup of the locally produced Nambarrie tea. We practiced for the annual Sports Day on those fields without anyone famous to cheer us on in the wheelbarrow race.

We had every reason to respect the gym because it was directly opposite the headmistress's study. This was a sacrosanct area of the school, and we automatically hushed our voices when we approached it. We had only two reasons to enter this holy place: as the last resort for the treatment of bad behavior (like the day Marion called a teacher "a silly sausage") or after receiving three *A*s or six *A*–s in a row. In the latter case, we lined up on the stairway with the notebook containing our *A*s, and Miss Lewis signed the book with a star. Occasionally, she would read through the work, but since the queue up the stair was long, her perfunctory star was the only contact we had with the headmistress. Yet her office was a wonderful oasis of warmth and comfort with its genuine coal fire and armchairs. Although these luxuries were not accessible to the girls, they were utopian symbols that offered the fleeting pleasure of standing in front of a warm fire until it was one's turn to receive a star.

The schoolyard was at the back of the building and could be seen from both the gym and the lab. Flanked by high brick walls, it offered only shelter. There was not enough space to play an organized game like rounders, so we simply chased one another aimlessly around the yard until tired, then drifted off to chat alongside the brick walls. A teacher was assigned to supervise these nonactivities, and when the bell rang, we formed yet another orderly queue and returned to the classrooms. When the weather was poor, which happened frequently, we were kept indoors, a welcome fate compared to random chases around the yard.

Princess Gardens School no longer exists. Yet the building, now used for offices of Queen's University, still stands in University Street, looking from the outside as solid and patrician as ever, displaying on the low wall a different brass sign. The boardinghouse has long since been converted into flats, and a smart-looking hotel has replaced the houses at the corner of the street. It might have been easier to return if the building had been demolished. That's what I thought when I finally crept back one late August day under heavy disguise as a mother of two teenagers. The secretary downstairs kindly allowed me to walk through the building, after I had explained my sentimental mission. They had taken down the walls and erected a flimsy-looking staircase with material that looked to me like plywood. All that remained of the building were the windows, but they looked empty without the heads peeping over the curtains on the second floor. Even had the girls all been there, there was nothing to look at, no sign of the blond sculptor, and not a single Morris Minor parked in the street.

Surely the presence of my children would soothe the pain of loss, but they were strangers and saw only a street of houses, so we headed toward Botanic Gardens. How could these young Americans ever understand their mother's tortured attachment to the deserted building around the corner? The elderly people on the park benches in Botanic Gardens would understand. Or did the way they stared at us suggest that we really did look like strangers? I would sit down for a bit of *craic* on the bench, and they would accept me as one of them, and the conversation would be as easy and aimless as chasing around in the school's backyard. Their presence would soothe away the years between and assure me that I had not forfeited the right to share a park bench with Belfast people in the shelter of Botanic Gardens, just around the corner from the actual building where I had learned to dissect the nasturtium that was already beginning to blossom with the promise of a rich autumn harvest.

4

The Teachers and What They Actually Taught

The teachers of Princess Gardens were all women, just as the pupils were all girls. The brown and fawn uniform that reduced the girls to carbon copies of one another was complemented by the attire of the teachers, all of whom wore an academic gown that concealed yet another layer of uniformity, namely, a worsted wool suit or skirt and twin set or combination of all three. The sensible brown laced shoes for the girls for outdoor wear and a brown strapped version for indoors resonated in the footwear of the teachers, which would have won the instant endorsement of the Royal Guild of Podiatrists, if such a society existed. Some teachers attempted to assert individuality by wearing a brooch, usually a simple marquisette cluster on the lapel of her suit. One teacher took striking risks with colorful scarves, but sadly they never matched the rest of the outfit, so at best her efforts looked like a bold fashion statement and at worst like the leftovers from a Bring and Buy sale.

Language conformity was not as immediately obvious as the dress code, but there were some subtle distinctions in the way they talked, which largely revealed their social class. Like the Harrison sisters, not a single teacher ever said aye in a public meeting, but dear knows what they said in the privacy of their chambers. There was a simple lexical test, efficient enough to pinpoint where one lived: how one used the word *dreadful*. If the reference was simply to the weather, then it was harmless. But if the adjective was attached to a person, it told you nothing about the person being spoken of—other than she/he did not belong—and everything you needed to know about the speaker. A weapon of class, *dreadful* was used by a teacher to separate herself from the masses and to assign to the slag heap of "dreadful" people those who had the gall to rise from the ranks. The most offensive "dreadfuls" were political rebels, especially Catholics. One elderly teacher—reared in a Presbyterian manse—had a nose for dreadful people like a beagle for hares, so that in the middle of an ordinary sentence she would suddenly come on the scent of a dreadful person, and her North Irish accent would immediately assume the tone of someone reared in an up-market borough of London, like Belgravia. In fact, a decently trained linguist with a specialty in phonetics could prove that the word used in tandem with *person* can only be uttered with an affected English accent. People up the Falls or the Shankhill do not call one another "dreadful." They use other words—much more interesting ones—but not *dreadful*. No farmer has ever been known in the history of the province—or indeed before 1921—to call another human being dreadful.

At a basic level the teachers of Princess Gardens were radical feminists, though they may not have represented themselves that way. For starters, they were completely and totally independent of men. No man was ever seen either on or near the school premises, except for Mr. Wilson who lived on the third floor. He would certainly not have been tolerated there, had he not been married to Mrs. Wilson, the school cook. A quiet, respectful man, he let himself in and out of the school and clearly knew his place. The other radical aspect of this community of women was a quite remarkable ability to preserve personal idiosyncrasies within a tightly structured unity. Every single one of them was radically different and as odd as two left feet, yet they did not maintain their individuality at one another's expense. Oddly enough, they all appeared to genuinely like one another. As far as we could ascertain, there was neither grandstanding nor jostling for prominence, and yet in all fairness the civility that they openly practiced had not produced a community of bores. The one exception was a gifted but exceptionally boring young teacher who attempted to draw the older girls into a harmless chat about the old-timers. Her attempt to win the hearts and minds of the sixth form met with instant rejection. Rumor had it that her mother was English.

One could argue that the harmony within the ranks of the teachers had a very simple explanation—they did not appear to hold staff meetings, historically the most virulent breeding ground for discord. But I suspect that their unity was based on the mutual agreement that in a benevolent dictatorship energy should not be expended quarreling among one another when they had the work of colonization to do among the girls. In case of rebellion in the ranks, two teachers held the working titles of junior mistress and senior mistress, but their jobs were to keep order among the girls and not among the mistresses. Besides, they had more important functions, like leading "The Lord's Prayer" and giving announcements at morning assembly.

The most immediate effect of teacher solidarity was the lack of a grievance procedure or recourse of any kind for the girls. If a teacher called a girl "a silly little ninny" for answering "two lemons" to the problem of how many days it would take ten men to mow three fields of wheat if it took one man eight hours, the student would get the same response—or worse—from the junior or senior mistress. That's the way it was. They all covered one another in a splendid impenetrable display of collegiality.

The declaration of independence from men was carried over into the private lives of the teachers. Unlike some contemporary feminists, these women did not drop their independent spirit the minute they passed the brass sign on the school wall. Few teachers were married. In fact, their confident attitude and deportment validated singleness as the better choice. Nor had they been corrupted by the cosmetic industry. Admittedly, it had not gained much of a footing in the community at large, but these women demonstrated a remarkable contempt for stereotypical notions of beauty. The local hair trend was ostentatious waves, achieved by clamping onto the hair medieval tongs that produced a very clever corrugated iron effect. As I recall, only one teacher succumbed to this coiffure, but she was married and had dandruff.

Had there ever been a staff meeting with pedagogical issues on the agenda, there is no doubt that the meeting would have lasted as long as it takes to say the word *memorization.* The notion of *educate,* meaning to "lead or bring out," had apparently been dismissed as too risky to use in Northern Ireland. Classroom discourse, dialectical debate—indeed, any kind of debate—were such remote concepts that had any teacher suggested them, she would have been suspected of being a socialist or worse. Our induction into the business of memorizing the known world began at an early age. Mathematical tables, simply called "tables," the Greek myths, simple French words, and poems in a book called *The Ring of Words* provided good fodder in first form. The assumption was that each pupil was a walking computer with storage capacity that expanded with age; the teacher's job was to punch in all the data, and the pupil would place it in the correct file. Some of us were better equipped to memorize than others. I, for one, had an older brother who subscribed to *Ring Magazine,* the most comprehensive boxing journal in the country. At an early age he introduced me to the joys of memorizing the featherweight champions of the United Kingdom, Europe, the world, and environs. From there on it was all downhill, what with the bantamweights, welterweights, and heavyweights just lounging along the ropes, waiting to be memorized. Low church girls who attended Mission Hall Sunday Schools, where they had to learn Bible verses weekly, also tended to distinguish themselves in the field of memorization.

The concept of memorization flourished without restraint in English class, where we had to learn several poems by heart each week. "Shall I compare thee to a summer's day" and its ilk were muttered on many a day en route from the bus stop in front of Queen's University all the way to University Street. Some lines have stuck, and all the therapists in the United States would be incapable of erasing Thomas Hardy's "What if still in chasmal beauty looms that wild weird western shore / The woman now is elsewhere whom the ambling pony bore, / And nor knows nor cares for Beeny, and will laugh there nevermore." But who in her right mind would want to forget Hardy's "Afterwards"? "When the present has latched its postern behind my tremulous stay, / And the May month flaps its glad green leaves like wings, / will the neighbours say, / 'He was a man who used to notice such things'? . . . If, when hearing that I have been stilled at last, they stand at the door, / Watching the full-starred heavens that winter sees, / Will this thought rise on those who will meet my face no more, / 'He was one who had an eye for such mysteries'?"

As a special treat we were occasionally allowed to choose a poem to memorize. The choices reflected the essential character of the girls, with the keen ones reciting endless dramatic monologues by Browning about well-bred, victimized women hanging on walls. Their zeal did not impress those of us who had cleverly found a delightful little poem about winter: "Every branch big with it / Bent every twig with it." I have forgotten who wrote it. Once more the battle lines tended to be drawn along denominational affiliation, with the Mission Hall girls and the merely cunning taking a well-deserved Sabbath rest.

The history teachers presented our greatest challenge in memorization, because the subject was presented as a succession of dates, loosely joined together by a series of wars, one of which lasted thirty years. This was, of course, in a different time and most definitely in a different place. We could be glad that our province did not have a history like that. In fact, in our classroom it did not appear to have any past at all. Our connection to the rest of the island was treated as a footnote to British history, and memorizing a couple of dates took care of our national identity. To know when King William crossed the Boyne was more important in the long run than to wonder why a Dutchman was riding over an obscure river in the Free State so far from home. The aim of the history teacher was to simply teach us the known world. The trick, of course, was to keep clear of the unknown. Nobody apologized for leaving us on the banks of the Boyne; the assumption was that we would make our own way home. And nobody warned us how painful the journey would be.

As I take out the green notebooks for history, I am compelled to acknowledge that the diligence of the teachers is inscribed on each page and that the array of facts and dates of British and European history are all in place—Gladstone's Irish policy is indeed there; the inadequacy of his first Irish Land Act of 1870; the effects of the Third Reform Bill of 1885, the one that extended the franchise to Ireland, resulting in "a vast increase of support for the Irish nationalist Party." The year 1910 is noted as the year in which home rule was a vital issue but was opposed "for religious and economic reasons. This opposition was exploited by the Conservative party." But there is no attempt to explain what these religious reasons were, and I certainly don't think we ever discussed it. Then a page later we meet the same James Craig whom my barefoot father had heard as a child in Blakeley's barn the night he followed the big Lambeg drums all the way to Drumbo. In my notes there are, of course, no bare feet, and the fiery speeches are represented as "intensified opposition led by Sir Edward Carson [appointed leader of the Unionists in 1910] and James Craig who set up a provisional government and controlled a volunteer army of extremists who broke away from the Irish Party; impending civil war was only averted by the outbreak of the First World War." My notes go on to point out that the third home rule bill was suspended for the duration of the war, "but the forces of the Gaelic League, the Labour movement directed by James Connally and Sinn Fein led by Arthur Griffith were already at work aiming at separation from Great Britain." I am afraid nobody, me included, asked where that left the likes of us. We simply kept on writing neatly into our green notebooks, without a word about Uncle Archie's contribution to the war effort in France.

Two pages suffice to cover the years immediately preceding 1922—including the insurrection of 1916, in which fifteen rebels were tried and shot. Apparently, republicanism had replaced "home rule" as the prevailing political force, and by 1918 the Republicans had won 73 of the 105 Irish votes. They refused to go to Westminster, declaring instead their allegiance to a republic under Eamon De Valera, and met in the Dail Eireann. In 1919 armed clashes occurred between the Republicans and "the forces of the Crown," followed in 1920 with the Government of Ireland Act, which provided for two parliaments, one in the North and one in the South. In the section entitled "British Democracy at War," I noted that "in May 1915 Asquith formed a coalition government (twelve liberals, eight Conservatives and one Labour) with Lloyd George as Minister of Munitions. Disagreements were frequent between politicians and the War Office and the death of Lord Kitchener, the Secretary for War in 1916, was a great loss." The next item listed under d) in my outline is "At

Easter 1916 a Sinn Fein rebellion in Dublin had to be put down."

I am not saying that knowing who the 1916 minister of munitions was is a useless piece of information or that Kitchener's death was *not* a great loss, especially to Mrs. Kitchener. It's the lineup that is problematic, for it suggests that what happened in d) was on a par with everything else in the world, even though it was happening a mere hundred miles up the road that led from Belfast—by way of Dromore, Newry, Dundalk, and Drogheda—to Dublin, and the suspicion is further confirmed by the next entry, which notes that the new war cabinet "included the Dominion Prime ministers, especially Smuts." Sticking a rebellion that happened a hundred miles away (two hours away by the Enterprise train) between the minister of munitions and Smuts was probably not a calculated ploy to alienate us from the history of the island where we had been born, but it had that effect—at least on one girl. The immediate goal was far more simple—to cover the assigned period, including the significant time lines of British history, like the First Afghan War from 1839 to 1849 under the administration of Governor General Lord Auckland and the annexation of the Punjab (1848–49), when "British power in India stretched as far as the mountains." We didn't ask which ones. (Maybe I remembered what happened when the Mulholland boy placed the Wicklow Mountains in Donegal.)

It was a photo finish between geography and history for memorization, with geography winning by a head.

Some countries were egregiously ignored, like the entire Far East and all the countries north of the Republic of South Africa. But we committed all the other countries of the colonized world to memory, along with their capital cities, main rivers, mountains, and industries, from Medicine Hat in Alberta (or was it Saskatchewan?) to pineapples flourishing in the tropical climate of Queensland. The geography teacher carefully drew on the blackboard a map of the region under scrutiny, which we then copied into our notebooks with the appropriate color, selected from the markers lined up on our desk. We then wrote her dictated notes into the same book under the headings—Relief, Climate, and Occupations. No girl ever was known to have lost a geography notebook, in the same way as no girl in my time ever lost a limb.

From the perspective of my adopted home in Wisconsin, it is sobering to read the section called "The Corn Belt." It certainly is a different angle on this part of the world, one that displays a rather inflated Lake Michigan, with Omaha and Cincinnati as major towns. A little brown blob west of Memphis shows the Ozark Plateau. Two large dots indicate that Chicago and Duluth are equal in size and importance. Milwaukee—"A great place on a great lake"—is conspicuous by its absence, but since Lake Michigan on my map is about as wide Texas, one should not quibble about Milwaukee's not being on it. Under the rubric "Towns and Industries" I recorded the following information: "The industries are mainly concerned with the processing of animal products. Every part of the animal is used, e.g. bones and blood for fertilizer." (It's a good thing my notebooks were not subpoenaed in the case that the Texas cattlemen brought against Oprah Winfrey.) Then comes a full paragraph about Chicago, without even mentioning Green Bay a few hundred miles up the same lake, a town that, even as we were transcribing information into our notebooks in Belfast, was home to a championship team that gave it the nickname "Titletown of America." Curiously enough, the description of Chicago comes right after the sentence that ends with "bones and blood for fertilizer" and I described it as follows: "Chicago is the most important city. It has enormous stockyards where the cattle are penned before being taken to the factories. It manufactures tinned meats, has bacon curing and makes lard etc. The city owes its importance to its situation at the southern-most end of the Great Lakes: Moreover, a glacial overflow channel provides an easy routeway for railways and canals from the lake to the Mississippi."

In all fairness, however, the role of cotton received excellent coverage: "Cotton requires a rich soil because it quickly exhausts soil. Therefore cotton growing within the belt is concentrated in three main areas. These are 1) Black (indecipherable word that looks like *waxy*) prairies of Texas; 2) Mississippi Flood Plain; 3) The Black belt of Alabama. Fertilizer can be had from Florida and from the Birmingham area. Cotton requires plentiful labour supply, since the bolls do not ripen at the same time. For this reason slaves were brought to America." Thus began and ended our exposure to and understanding of the slave trade.

The transcribing into notebooks with the name PRINCESS GARDENS SCHOOL clearly marked on the front green cover was the central activity of the school. These exercise books were made for eternity. Uncorrupted by pupils' suggestions, they contained the definitive statement of each teacher's knowledge of her subject. Unlike the common jotter, they were not the repository of adolescent musings but would be part of each girl's baggage when she left the school. With their historical value in view, the green books were frequently collected and carefully examined by each teacher for neatness. A messy green book's being discovered in a future epoch, maybe in a foreign land, was a sobering thought.

The subject of testing a pupil's response to the green book is another chapter in the history of the school. There was, of course, no such thing as multiple choice or filling in a blank. The very idea of such a method would have met with the first staff meeting ever called in the history of the school and certainly would have been dismissed as the work of a complete ninny. Final exams, however, were a shocking surprise and a challenge to every notion of memorization mentioned earlier.

The essay questions that we had to tackle during exam week embodied the lowest imaginable form of teacher cunning and gave new meaning to the phrase "hidden agenda." Suddenly, we had to comment on the complexities of theme and motif in poems that had heretofore been understood simply as "Every branch big with it." We had to give "pen portraits" of Jane Austen characters and intricacies of plots. Mathematical problems involving scores of men mowing acres of hay were given for ratios and the nearest square foot to the nearest mile. The impertinent questions in history had less to do with cherished dates than analysis but still were as far away from home as possible. The most naive among us began to suspect from the questions that there were actually patterns in historical events that we were suddenly supposed to spot and "write lucidly on the above." Nothing was predictable any more. The five-day examination period at the end of each term was the school's threshing week, when the really clever girls were winnowed out as wheat, separated irrevocably from the rest of us, who were now publicly exposed as the school's chaff, little ninnies nourished on *Ring Magazine,* reeling under punches that we had not been trained to meet.

5
The Explosion

No class generated more terror in the hearts of some of us than science. We were easy to identify as a group, for we sat at the low end of the table, perched on high stools that we pushed close together in the hope of finding a crumb of comfort in the physical proximity of girls who were equally hopeless in science and equally despised by Mrs. Carr, though not necessarily for lack of gift. The instruction of science had always been torture, despite disguising it as botany in the lower forms. At an age when we should have been acting out "Up the airy mountain, down the rushy glen," or making a collage of wildflowers, we were learning how to dissect a nasturtium under clinical conditions that would satisfy the U.S. Centers for Disease Control.

We all had to bring our sample flowers to class in a brown bag, which was then opened in full view of Mrs. Carr, who supervised the dissection, identifying the public and private parts of the poor little flower that was already visibly wilting under our hot little fingers. It was no fun, especially when your flower had barely survived the seven-thirty bus ride. Some girls loved it, showing off their dissecting skills like they were headed for a career as a neurosurgeon. I was not among the latter. Delicate petals were torn asunder and the exposed parts identified by means of an underlined arrow. I have long since forgotten the names that we wrote under the arrows, but I can still see the orange and yellow petals helplessly pinned down on the unlined pages of our notebooks. The successful dissection of the nasturtium was celebrated by an outing to the Botanic Gardens, around the corner from the school, where we would visit the greenhouse that housed exotic plants and flowers like palms and orchids. We had barely time to take off our coats upon our return to school before the excursion was written up in the green notebook, again under the beady eye of Mrs. Carr. "On Monday Mrs. C. (very kindly) took Upper Fourth to Botanic park." (I do not know when the parentheses were inserted. I am sure I did it.)

The next level of science was astronomy, which anyone in her right mind might assume would be a great adventure. I knew the sky already, or thought I did until I entered the classroom, for where I lived—far from city lights—the Plough, Cassiopeia, Cepheus, the Swan and the Lyre, and all the other constellations bent over backward to put on a spectacular show over the hills of Ballycoan, especially during harvest time, when the moon vied for top billing. The stories behind the stars relieved the monotony of the class somewhat, especially the one about Pegasus, the wonderful horse with silvery wings that carried its rider far away from the earth, away up into the upper sunny air. (Maybe the expressionist Franz Marc was fueled by the same stories when he painted those magnificent horses for the poet Else Lasker-Schüler.)

We learned that Pegasus came back to Earth, where the dull country folk failed to recognize him. You had to wonder if Mrs. Carr herself would not have been among the latter group, as intent as she appeared to be on divesting the stars of wonder and lining them all up so they wouldn't fall. For me there was nothing more magical than to walk up the lane with my mother on a starlit night and hear her say, "You could pick pins and needles tonight." I never questioned the logic of why anyone had lost their pins and needles in the first place, but it was comforting to know that if that happened, there would be nights so sparkling and clear that the distraught person would find every single pin and needle that had been lost—glistening in the middle of the lane from the light of the stars.

But that's not how Mrs. Carr viewed the galaxies. She liked to carve them up into sections of the sky and measure their angles. In and of itself, this indeed is a great way to earn a living. I might have become a good astronomer if Mrs. Carr had been more patient with me. But she did not conceal her impatience and disapproval of my night sky, one that was filled with constellations hanging at perilous angles to the earth. Furthermore, in exams I could remember only that when Perseus and Andromeda died, Athena took them up into the sky and that on starlight nights you can still see them, especially Andromeda, spreading her long white arm across the heavens. (And I learned that from Charles Kingsley.) I can think of few moments in life more demoralizing than to have your galaxies publicly mocked—and by a woman who wore a brooch.

The next levels of science were chemistry and physics, the latter such a total disaster that I cannot retrieve any memory of any class. Chemistry, however, has left a certain residue and an explosion that will culminate presently. As a collective experience chemistry classes have all flowed together over the years into one gigantic Bunsen burner. Everything that we did in the lab ended up on a Bunsen burner. Yet in more rational moments I know this is not true. For the ultimate proof— the green notebook—indicates that the Bunsen burner was not even mentioned when we heated blue vitriol, nor when we found the percentage of water from crystallization in different samples of blue vitriol. Had I been teaching about blue vitriol, I would have sabotaged the whole experiment with poetry examples, like Else Lasker-Schüler's poem "My Blue Piano." The first lines are, "I have a blue piano in my house / I am not able to play." Then I would have talked about the color blue and told the class what Kandinsky thought of sorrow as being deep blue—all this in the hope that colors would not be dissolved over a Bunsen burner.

Take, for example, the quest to find the percentage of sal ammoniac (ammonium chloride) in a mixture of sand, salt, and sal ammoniac. A crucible is weighed, a few grams of the mixture are added, and the crucible is weighed again. The crucible is then heated, gently at first and then more strongly. The main player in the experiment is the Bunsen burner, providing the heat that leads to the sublimation in the crucible. Whether examining the gas given off when potassium chlorate is heated, whether heating zinc or lead, the method—at least in my memory—always involves the Bunsen burner. Consider, for example, the effect of heat on sulfur. It decrepitates slightly and then melts to a yellow mobile liquid. It first becomes light amber, then dark amber, then suddenly so viscous that the test tube can be inverted without the sulfur running out. As the temperature rises still further, the color then deepens even more, becoming such a dark red that it appears to be almost black, and the liquid becomes mobile once again. The molten sulfur boils, and some of it passes into vapor, which condenses on the cold sides of the test tube to a pale yellow powder, known as flowers of sulfur. It should, therefore, be clear that there can be no conversion, no calces, no ashes without a flame, and the provider of that flame will always be the Bunsen burner.

There are also few connections in my education between chemistry and chemists—the men or women who came to such startling conclusions—that, for example, finely powered sulfur is sparingly soluble in cold water. The people who discovered that a metal increases in mass when heated (no doubt using you-know-what kind of burner) because it absorbs some air—did they write letters or poetry? I suppose I should be grateful for a couple of names attached to the ubiquitous burners, like a chemist called Joseph Priestley, who on August 1, 1774, heated the red calx of mercury by focusing the sun's rays upon it, using a fine burning glass that had just come into his possession. To his amazement the calx gradually changed into mercury and the residual gas supported combustion vigorously. A mouse lived longer in it than it would have in the same volume of air. And I also hasten to add that Priestley contacted the French chemist Antoine-Laurent Lavoisier, who repeated Priestley's experiment, confirmed the results, and called the new gas "eminently breathable," which seems a lot more lyrical than plain old oxygen. I am ashamed to write that we did not discuss the uses (and certainly not the abuses or potential abuses) that these discoveries were put to. I recall a few lame references to artificial manure, refrigeration, and solvents for grease, but even these are quickly absorbed by the recurring phrase in the green book—"unpleasant odour"—and especially by the pervasive presence of the Bunsen burner.

The incident—I should say, event—that I want to write about was extraordinary, even though it took place in the same lab where flowers were dismantled and stars were bossed around in the ubiquitous presence of a Bunsen burner. It happened on a day that may have looked like any other day, but this one would be different. We were lined up in our usual order, with the two favorites flanking Mrs. Carr and the rest of us seated in descending order of intelligence and confidence to the small, tightly knit group that was cowering at the nether end of the long table. The hierarchy of seating arrangement was the least scientific aspect of the spotlessly kept lab. While the girls at the top brought to the lab acceptable mathematical aptitude, they possessed nonscientific attributes that the group at the other end simply could not match. They did not have to catch the four o'clock bus. This, more than any other factor, marginalized us girls at the end of the table. We were country girls who did not come and go at the whim of our feet or of a city bus. We were totally dependent on the four o'clock. This dependence had drawn us into a primitive form of support group, a fellowship of suffering that sustained us during the long hours before science, typically the last two periods of the day.

For us the four o'clock bus was not just a means of conveyance but a chariot of deliverance that took us back to where we belonged, back to the moist warmth of cow byres (barns), to the drone of threshing machines on autumn days, and to the aroma of wheaten bread baked on the griddle. The four o'clock delivered us from the tyranny of the little white sandwiches that city mothers packed for their girls in clean brown bags, as opposed to our crusty wheaten bread wrapped in the obituary page of the *Belfast Telegraph*. Thus missing the four o'clock was to be deprived of reconnection with the vitality of life that five o'clock tea in the comfort of a County Down farm kitchen alone can offer.

We had every reason to dread missing the four o'clock. Mrs. Carr gave oral tests capriciously, and the girls at the end of the table were the first victims of detention. The ritual was as unpleasant as the lumps in the mincemeat of school dinners. The trouble was, and I suppose still is, that chemical formulae look and sound so dangerously related. Just add an extra *o* or *h* in your answer, and you have plutonium instead of plain water. And invariably, the girls who had to catch the four o'clock came up with the most explosive answers. Nor did it help when one of us would melt into hysterical titters at the other's pitifully incorrect answer. Then all of us (with the exception of the girls at the top end) were castigated as complete ninnies. No amount of time spent beside the tilly lamp (an oil lamp) the night before seemed to help. The anguish of missing the four o'clock was a prospect that made it scientifically impossible to memorize chemical formulae.

I have never been able to understand my love affair with autumn. Even using the American word *fall* deprives the season of not a drop of its beauty. Everything that I hold beautiful is framed by the shapes and smells of autumn. It is as if the sun had been practicing all year to get the angle perfect and now finally has figured it out. People, even children, do not seem as loud in autumn. I am about to describe a lovely day, so it must have taken place in autumn. I am forced to invoke an autumn day in Wisconsin, in order to have a perfect frame, for in all honesty there is little difference between a summer or even a winter day in Northern Ireland, but this is much too grand a day to insert in a drab frame, so we shall—in the spirit of the German poet Rilke—"Command the last fruits to incarnadine"—infuse a more southerly day into the text, enflame it with an imported sun, so that the nasturtium growing in profusion in the Botanic Gardens around the corner can assume a more golden hue, for it was a perfect day.

Mrs. Carr entered the lab as usual, that is, wearing a brooch, her personal insignia of elegance, and announced that she was going to perform an experiment for the two full periods; we were to sit quietly on top of the table and observe. The hierarchy and oppression that had shaped the table were instantly obliterated by this declaration of emancipation. We scrambled on top of the table, Rosetta girls—city girls who didn't have to catch the four o'clock bus—cheek by jowl with girls from farms near Comber, bonded in a unity that transcended bus schedules.

It was soon clear that even Mrs. Carr had entered into the spirit of the afternoon. Her usually condemning countenance held not a trace of disapproval. Each eager face received an equal portion of her attention as she carefully explained the details of the experiment at hand. Methodically analyzing the properties of each ingredient in her experiment, she carefully lined up her paraphernalia. Our awe and expectancy grew by the second. I have no idea, nor did I then, what the experiment was meant to prove or disprove. But I do remember with absolute clarity that Mrs. Carr forewarned us that there would probably be a terrific bang. (And that's the reason, she explained, that we were sitting on top of the table, well away from the experiment yet with unobstructed view.) This was clearly science at its best, if at its most dangerous. Freed from the worry of missing the four o'clock, because this departure from routine meant no surprise tests that afternoon, we were completely focused on Mrs. Carr's experiment while basking in our new freedom, admittedly in a limited sense, because the full import of an anxiety-free science class would not set in, at least for some of us, for several decades.

By the tense look on Mrs. Carr's face, we could expect the dénouement any second. She had filled the scales with fine powder, set the scales over Bunsen burners, and lined up vials filled with different hues. We could be blown out of Northern Ireland into eternity at any moment. We were positively hanging by our toenails over the edge of the table, clinging with apocalyptic terror to the girl beside us, who could be anybody in this new world order. There was no turning back for any of us, but especially not for Mrs. Carr, who may have chosen that route, given what happened next. Nothing happened, unless you call a little fizzle an explosion. I do not remember how Mrs. Carr reacted. But I do remember the look of absolute mirth that transformed the green eyes of a very quiet girl who always sat with us country girls at the bottom of the table. She was from Belfast and therefore did not have to catch the four o'clock. But she was Pentecostal.

6

La Porte Étroite

The freedom of having hills and valleys to play in as children severely restricted our interest in the world and in people beyond our world. If they came to visit, it was an intrusion, especially in summer when the evenings were so long you could play on the hills for hours, chasing one another in and out of the hay bales half the night, and yet still see a sliver of sun. A second cousin of my father's visited once from Hingham, Massachusetts, and must have thought that we were deprived, for, after returning to the United States, she sent a doll for my sister and me. It was probably an early ancestor of the Barbie doll, a grotesque creature and another intrusion on our playtime. My sister wisely suggested that we drag it though the sheugh at the bottom of the hill to soften the wretched thing up a bit. Although badly soiled and lame in one leg, it was a lot more flexible, but we quickly tired of it and went back to playing. Our mother said it was a good thing the American relative couldn't see what we had done to it, for she might think we were destructive. Our mother often said wise things like that.

We had several intrusions into our childhood from foreigners, some, like Chantal, my sister's pen pal, more welcome than others. The ones from Finland could have been a disaster, had we not taken the matter into our own hands. Two young Finnish women came to live with us during two successive summers as au pairs. One was called Ritva Blick, and the other one's first name was Saya with a last name that sounded something like Ratakina—I'm just taking a stab at it. When the Finnish women finally realized that summer bedtime hours for children on a farm were a contradiction in terms, they gave up and joined us till all hours of the night. Ritva's family had a cottage up in Lapland, and by the stories she told us it sounded like a right (fine) place to go and fish. Saya was a city woman so her stories were less interesting, except for the one about making a bathing suit out of a swastika flag during the war, but we didn't know what a swastika meant then, so the story was a bit pointless. All we could think was it must have been a quare size of a flag, for she was powerful hefty.

Chantal was to become and remain a lifelong family friend. She had corresponded for several years with my sister in a pen pal exchange arranged through school and finally accepted our invitation to spend three weeks at Ash Hill. From the day she arrived, you would have thought she had been reared at the top of the Ballycoan Road. Our first clue that this teenager from Villeneuve St. Georges near Paris was not fancy was the way she tucked into the wheaten farls, smothering them with butter and black currant jam. When it came to bread, we either baked it or had it delivered. But we had seen pictures of Frenchmen with big long loaves of bread tied to the backseat of their bike and knew we couldn't provide either the shape of bread or the men to pick it up at the bakery. Billy Miskelly came to the door with his bread van every other day, but even his long hook could not pull out from the back of the van the kind of bread you saw on French postcards. Granted, he had baps (small rolls) called Paris buns, which were about as Parisian as he was, and Veda bread made with malt, but Chantal stuck with the wheaten farls and over the years wrapped them up in damp tea towels to bring home to Villeneuve St. Georges.

Another interesting surprise for us was Chantal's reaction to the murals of King Billy that were painted on the sides of houses in East Belfast with slogans like "No Pope Here." Our dad tried hard to avoid driving near those streets, especially during the Twelfth fortnight, the two weeks of holiday following the mid-July commemoration of the Battle of the Boyne. But as much as he tried, there they were—blazingly orange on the sides of terraced houses, announcing to our guest from France that the head of her church was persona non grata and had better not come to our province for his holidays. Curiously enough, Chantal was more amused than offended by the slogans, and what is even more astonishing, she liked our bachelor uncles and even fancied our bookish cousin with his National Health glasses and zero interest in playing in hay bales. We had forewarned her about certain oddities in the household of our uncles. One barely spoke. The other hunched over his wireless set in the hope of picking up weather forecasts, and, though he had never even been in a row boat, he listened to shipping forecasts about far-flung places like the Dogger Bank, all in the hope that he could micromanage the wilderness he called his garden. Chantal found both men interesting and kind. The word *odd* never left her lips. We were forced to look again at the tall frail cousin who was too serious to play in the bales. Chantal liked him, was impressed that he spoke French well enough to converse with her about Racine, and found him attractive. We were shocked.

But summer ended, and we had to go back to school to experience a much more significant assault on the narrowness of our life. It came this time in the shape of a Parisian, not someone from a *banlieu* of Paris. Our school and Miss Crone, the French and German teacher who was my mentor, had embarked on an ambitious plan to bring French—and at a later phase German—to us, since the chances of any of us ever going abroad were slim, considering that some of us had never been to Coleraine, a town only forty miles from Belfast. The woman who arrived on the school's doorstep at the beginning of term was simply called Mademoiselle. The headmistress introduced her to the school in morning assembly, and then Miss Crone escorted her, with the dignity worthy of such an occasion, to meet us girls in the classroom upstairs. Miss Crone was tall but not in a dreary, undernourished way. She looked nothing like Chantal, who was petite and vivacious. It just shows you how stereotypes can let you down. So it does. But Mademoiselle didn't have to be vivacious, for she had a presence and poise about her that defied description. Physically, she was a regular Brünhilde, with massive shoulders on a sturdy body that would have been the envy of any male sergeant in the Royal Marines. We took to her instantly. And she reciprocated by falling about in mirth at both our French and our English. She loved us, called us *charming,* a word that had never been used before—or probably since—on any of us. We were witty and amusing; our French was delightful, and our dialect—this was news to us-was much more "gai" than BBC English.

But her greatest achievement was to open our eyes to Northern Ireland. On the weekends Mademoiselle would hitchhike all over Ireland, thumbing lifts from lorry drivers going to Galway and Cork. Her forays into the South fortunately did not change her mind about us in the North. Frankly, we knew that when she discovered Dublin, that would be the end of us and our charm. This fear proved to be no more than an adolescent eruption of Northern Irish paranoia. Dublin was indeed "gai," but Belfast was also amusing, had character and its own identity, and Mademoiselle drew out untapped loyalty to a working-class town. She loved the shipyards and pointed out the symmetry of the Victorian streets and the treasures that they hid, years before it was fashionable to take a photo of the Crown

Bar in Great Victoria Street. She took photographs of men in duncher caps, the peaked caps of the laborers whom we would have been ashamed to acknowledge as relatives. Mademoiselle selected the little town of Hillsborough as "un village charmant" thirty years before its merchants started to hang petunias outside specialty shops that sell aromatic candles.

Mademoiselle not only made us aware that we were from Irlande du Nord, she prepared us to enter the European Union long before Margaret Thatcher ever thought of arguing against it. Our identity had been stretched and redefined, with the result that we could feel at ease in Paris and Munich or even in villages like St. Tulle in Provence or Harburg in Bavaria. The world was turning out to be not nearly as far away as we thought it was, and we could go there and not make total fools of ourselves. We had always innocently assumed that Paris was France. Miss Crone had read Alphonse Daudet's *Lettres de Mon Moulin* to us, but we were much too astute to take it as a serious description of France; it was an idyll, a French Sunday School excursion to the provinces. Those wee *cigales* chirping in the hot sun didn't fool us. Paris was still France.

I am not sure how Paris had captivated our hearts, possibly from a perfume called Evening in Paris that was available at Littlewoods, the local dime store. The perfume came in a very attractive blue bottle that could function in a decent Proustian revelation as a lavatory cleanser. But the packaging and name were glamorous and exemplified sophistication. It was, therefore, a bit of a shock when Mademoiselle reduced Paris to its historic buildings, with the exception of the Eiffel Tower and Sacre Coeur, which apparently were horrors. True Parisians did not live there; Paris was essentially a postal address, and the *maison de campagne* was the real home of the French. The charm of a country house was lost on those of us who lived in one in the hills and valleys around Belfast. Certainly, from the way some teachers treated the country girls, you would never have guessed that they lived in a *maison de campagne*. The very idea that city people, especially Parisians, might choose to live in Ballycoan or Moneyreagh was a discovery, offering the remote possibility that those drafty old farmhouses might have an inherent worth that Malone Road people had missed.

So Paris was demolished as the cultural capital of Europe, but an interesting alternative replaced it. We were mesmerized to hear that Europe's best-kept architectural secret was a town called Bruges. I now recognized that my dreams of exploring the streets of Montmartre were bourgeois, a word that Mademoiselle loved and taught us to use correctly. It took us ages to find Bruges on the map because it turned out to be in Belgium and not in France at all. Though no bigger on the map than Portadown, Bruges had won our vote as the undiscovered gem of Europe, at least for people like Mademoiselle and us, who had eyes to see. We did not know then that she had shaped our cultural tastes for life.

The most subversive aspect of Mademoiselle's school activities, however, was her taste in literature. You could see it right in front of your nose, for no one ever flaunted literary tastes like Mademoiselle. Except she didn't know she was flaunting anything—even the Gitane cigarettes that topped her large canvas bag, right beside paperback books with provocative titles like *L'Immoraliste* by a man called André Gide. We asked her about this book, because it didn't sound like the ones we were reading with Miss Crone, like *Servitude et Grandeur Militaire* by Alfred de Vigny, and certainly not like the lugubrious poem "Le Lac" by Lamartine that we were wading thorough. We had also embarked on several tedious poems by de Vigny that used up several vocabulary notebooks. Miss Crone read "Le Lac" aloud to us, infusing every line with such emotion that she brought tears to her eyes. We struggled to keep up but never were quite proficient enough to even feign a sad look, never mind cry. Mademoiselle was glad to fill in some blanks in our knowledge of French literature—we thought the French writers had closed up shop when de Vigny died in 1863. Apparently, Gide had written what sounded like a companion piece to *L'Immoraliste* called *La Porte Étroite,* about the tortured love between two cousins that is as pious as the other story is carnal. This man not only wrote about struggles with straight gates and narrow ways, but he also chose a title for one straight from the Gospels—"Except a grain of wheat fall into the ground and die." Gide called it *Si le Grain Ne Meurt,* and Mademoiselle translated the title for us matter-of-factly, without falling about laughing just because it came from the Bible. (We had confined it rigidly within a religious setting, but here it was on the cover of a book—and a French book at that.) When she came to the bit about Gide's being a Protestant, that did it. Of course, we knew there were Protestants in France—who wouldn't after that desperate massacre in Paris we read about with Miss Crone?—but the way Mademoiselle used the word was different somehow. The word was not used in relation to or opposed to anything else. That's what was new. It wasn't going to start a riot. He was protestant, probably with a small *p* and so were we—just like André Gide. Except he was from France and we were from Irlande du Nord.

7

"Du Kommst Nie Wieder"—You Will Not Come Back

Miss Crone loved literature. Though a respected teacher, she was primarily and passionately engaged in literature. Her goal was to introduce the girls of Princess Gardens School, Belfast, to the joys of reading in French, German, and Latin, the three languages she had mastered with great distinction, and to share the joys of a literature that lay beyond tedious chapters on the subjunctive and prepositions that took the accusative or the dative (at the whim, it seemed to us, of some primitive Germanic tribe). Miss Crone made no bones about her impatience in seeing her goal come to fruition and introduced us in the lower sixth form, during our high adolescence, to the nineteenth-century Novelle in German and to the French Romantic poets, with Lamartine and Alfred de Vigny the clear front-runners.

The class size by this time had shrunk to a half-dozen, all of us in the front row with nowhere to hide in the anguished struggle to find a verb in one of those endless German sentences. We took turns reading and then translated our way laboriously through the texts. Miss Crone quite sensibly ignored the intrusion of our own low-slung palates into the French and German.

She never ridiculed our pronunciation or attempted to raise the level of local vowels. A few girls rolled their French *r* quite remarkably, but Miss Crone's solemn face registered neither approval nor curiosity as to where on Earth they had picked up the habit. It was certainly not from her, for though fluent in both languages she clearly had resisted any attempt to compromise her own rich North Irish accent. Therefore, homegrown vowels, no matter how low they clung, or how thoroughly they betrayed our roots, were not and never would be perceived by Miss Crone as an impediment in the learning of a foreign language. The discovery of literature was, in a nutshell, Anne Crone's reason to learn a language.

Miss Crone's theory of language acquisition rested squarely on the grammar-based / lexical list approach, a method that has long since been discredited and replaced by the communicative approach, which certainly equips students to function better than my generation after landing at an airport or a train station. I am not sure whether Miss Crone would ever have rethought the pedagogy of second-language acquisition. It is impossible for me to imagine her working with videos or computerized learning, for her approach to teaching centered on memorization. This meant that in the lower third form we were already learning verb conjugations in all three languages. Then Miss Stiles took over Latin, and Miss Crone reigned supreme over French and German.

We foolishly thought that Latin would be money for jam on the day we memorized *amo, amas, amat,* etc., but we were brought back to Earth when we hit the next conjugation. In French the vocabulary lists became progressively more detailed, but in German the verbs had taken a terrible turn for the worse. French nouns, particularly the vocabulary of the theater and of the garden shed, included every word that pertained to every nook and cranny, every curtain, nuance of tassel, every trowel and pruning hook that civilization has ever known. That some girls had never set foot in a theater in our own province was irrelevant; we had a complete list stored in our head if the opportunity ever arose to use it in France. And even if we didn't, it would come in handy when we read a novel in French that had to do with the theater or indeed a garden shed. I suspect that the assumption that shaped the theory of second-language acquisition in the whole province was that any language on Earth can, and frankly should, be enjoyed in the privacy of the home, preferably by a coal fire.

I remember how impressed we were when Miss Crone casually announced that she had read a wonderful Novelle the night before—*Das Amulett* by the Swiss writer Conrad Ferdinand Meyer. It was to be our next assignment. We could look forward to reading about the Troubles in sixteenth-century France, when French Huguenots were slaughtered on the streets of Paris in the Massacre of St. Bartholomew's Night. Of course, Miss Crone didn't represent the book that way. She was too caught up in the plot about a Swiss Protestant's friendship with a Swiss Catholic, who saved the Protestant from certain death by sneaking a medallion into his clothing, deftly placing it right in front of his heart. (The Catholic had been able to accomplish this in the middle of a long embrace.) You could tell that Miss Crone was all excited about introducing us to this story and was acting like we wouldn't sleep in our beds that night in anticipation of discussing its contents. And she had read it in an evening. I, for one, gave up after the first two paragraphs, having already used up half my green vocabulary notebook before I had even met the Catholic. If he was as boring as the Protestant I had met among the big words on the first page, he would need the medallion himself.

By the time we had reached the lower sixth, we had memorized every noun in *Larousse* and knew that German used some highfalutin verb form to express wishes/desires. We had learned to place our verbs at the end of a subordinate clause and that, if you had an auxiliary verb, you put it right at the end. Obviously, you quickly learned to avoid using any helping verb in the past tense. In fact, as a general rule, you avoided any reference to the past. We were also taught how to express a subjunctive in the past tense, as in "If I had wanted to do that, I would have." This was a shock because the verb lineup was arbitrarily changed, and now we were told that we had to (this was *not* an option) put our helping verb first in the verb lineup. It was enough to push you over the edge. We had also entered into the second phase of the foreign language program and had acquired another European, this time a young woman from Germany, whom we addressed as Fräulein. She was at least six feet tall, and no amount of imagination or charity could attribute a single attractive feature to the gaunt face, whose pallor was accentuated by greasy brown hair that twisted across her head in skinny plaits. A drab dress and laced shoes complete my memory of a woman with the least merry heart I have ever known. I am sure that an interesting and maybe even exciting woman was hiding under the exterior, but we were unable to elicit anything from her other than a vague but pervasive expression of reproach. Nothing about us pleased her. I had the misfortune of having to spend a whole hour with her in the school music room, where the only claim to comfort was two hard chairs and an upright piano, a setting that Fräulein probably found *gemütlich*. My first encounter with her, when I read a poem by Goethe, provoked an immediate frontal attack on my vowels. Before the hour was over, the consonant system that had flourished wild and free under the civil tongue of Miss Crone lay shattered. But there was worse to come. Fräulein decided after two sessions to teach me to write. Somewhere in Germany a well-meaning teacher had instructed her that an essay had to have a beginning, a middle, and an ending. She had taken this innocent suggestion to heart and now was trying to fob it off on Northern Ireland. One day, en route to an oral exam at Victoria College in Miss Crone's highly polished motor car, an Austin "A Thirty" that looked even then like a collector's item, I shamelessly exposed Fräulein's plot. Miss Crone was too noble a woman to betray her true feelings toward this blitz on my spoken and written German, but her kind gray eyes held the suggestion of laughter. She also gave me permission to cut back on the classes with Fräulein.

In the German literature class with Miss Crone, however, our crude little sensibilities were being slowly refined by a novel called *Immensee* by Theodor Storm. It is about a young couple called Reinhardt and Elisabeth, who love and lose each other. Elisabeth is wooed by a lad called Erich, an eager suitor and best friend of Reinhardt's. Reinhardt had neglected Elisabeth when he was away at university, and after a bit of a fling with a gypsy girl, he returns to find that Elisabeth has meanwhile married his boring friend. They live childless on a grand estate with lake and vineyard—probably not far from the Jewish cemetery in Harburg that we'll visit later—and the old mother dragging around with the house keys, a symbolic touch that Miss Crone was quick to point out showed who was still the boss. Reinhardt, now a fully grown man, visits the estate at Immensee, and after staying there for an undisclosed time, quietly lets himself out of the house, bag and baggage, one glorious early autumn morning, cleverly positioned at the end of the Novelle. Elisabeth appears at the top of the stairs, pauses, and then pronounces the grand finale—that he will never come back, except she said it in German—"Du kommst nie wieder." Neither moves; then Reinhardt abruptly leaves, heading for, as the German puts it, "die große, weite Welt." The reader is then returned from "the big wide world" to the original frame of the story, which portrays Reinhardt as a lonely old bachelor-scholar, sitting in his armchair one autumn afternoon; the story within the frame turns out to be a reminiscence of his love. This was noble stuff for teenagers at an all-girls school, and Miss Crone presented the story without reference to the possibility of irony or sentimentality. Life might turn out that way for any one of us. Maybe it had for her. Some of us would never come back. And dear knows what lay ahead in that big, wide world out there beyond our own North Irish Immensees.

We should have suspected that Miss Crone's total immersion in the books she read to and with us was more than the zeal of a teacher or the interest of a dilettante. We were so impressed that she read books that it never occurred to any of us that she wrote them, until her first novel, *Bridie Steen,* was published. We were also too insensitive and thick to ascribe significance to the preoccupied dreamy look in her eyes at lunchtime. And I was the worst culprit, for I sat right at her table and had no idea that she was inventing plots and imagining scenes in the bogs of Fermanagh while we were all choking down the mincemeat dinner. Nor did her literary activities ever impinge upon the classroom, where it was business as usual, garden sheds and all. The rumor that *Bridie Steen* was a love story was substantiated one day, when an excited girl produced a copy of the book and read aloud an excerpt about an embrace close enough for the heroine to actually feel the fountain pen in the top pocket of the man's jacket. We were too shocked and delighted that Miss Crone was capable of such a risqué love scene to comprehend the much more significant risk that she had taken in the fifties. *Bridie Steen* was the story of a love relationship between a Catholic and a Protestant. Few of us had read beyond the opening line—"The bog was beautiful"—but we had managed to find the juicy bit. What also eluded us was that Wordsworth had provided the titles for her next two novels—*My Heart and I* and *This Pleasant Lea.* Miss Crone was, after all, the modern languages mistress, and English poetry was the domain of the English mistress.

It would take years for me to grasp that Miss Crone had found in her field of scholarly interest a narrow gate that opened up to a much wider world, one that would lead her back to the bogs of Fermanagh where she had spent her childhood. No Irish writer, man nor woman, has captured the magic of those bogs like Anne Crone. Was she aware at the time that she had provided the keys that we would use to make our own discoveries, our own connections with people and places beyond our narrow province? Anne Crone died of a heart attack in Belfast some years ago. I regret to say that I do not know exactly when. *Bridie Steen* was reprinted by Blackstaff Press in the eighties. At the time of her death she was still teaching modern languages at Princess Gardens. That is all I know, for over the years I neglected to keep in touch with her, fearing that my own literary tastes were so far removed from *Immensee* and "Le Lac" that we would have little to say to each other. But I often mention her in my introduction to German literature class at the University of Wisconsin in Milwaukee and on one occasion actually allowed a student to borrow my green vocabulary notebook inscribed with PRINCESS GARDENS SCHOOL when he was struggling with the vocabulary of *Das Amulett*. So on this quiet autumn day in Wisconsin, I pause with deep regret and wistfulness to recapture belatedly the memory of a remarkable woman who passionately loved our province. She also protected one of its children from those who insist that a story must have an ending.

8

No Luster of Our Own

We officially heralded the dawn of a new school day by assembling in the gym, within steps of the headmistress's office. The headmistress was escorted to the gym by the head girl, who quietly informed her of the hymn number, both fulfilling one of their most important public functions. The younger girls participated in a less mature version of the assembly in the other wing of the building under the junior mistress, who was informed of the hymn number by a senior prefect. When the headmistress was not in residence, the senior mistress presided over assembly. She too was informed of the hymn number by the head girl but with less ceremony.

The solemnity and formality of the daily assembly were foreshadowed by the stationing of prefects at the bottom and top of each staircase on the three floors of the school. Ideally, their stern faces should have sufficed to remind the girls that they were to be silent en route to and from the assembly. Sadly, their demeanor was not always a deterrent to the more rebellious, and occasionally a girl had to be taken out of the procession and placed beside the prefect. There she stood, a blushing reminder to all of the authority of a prefect and the sheer folly of indulging in one's fallen nature

We filed reverently into the gym, the senior girls moving to the back of the room and the others ranked according to their form, with the youngest girls right under the nose of the headmistress. The teachers sat along the wall closest to the platform in order of a seniority that flowed in a seamless hierarchy from the most senior teacher to the most recent appointees, with a photo finish in seat rank between two young women near the door who looked no older than some of the sixth formers, at least the ones with boyfriends. Miss Crone sat next to the platform and could have touched the vaulting horse on the platform had she wanted to make a public display of her superior rank. The prefects flanked the wall at the lower end of the gym in a similar if more self-conscious caste system, given the dirty looks they shot at any girl with the suggestion of mischief in her eyes. All the girls had to stand during the entire assembly, which seemed like eternity if the headmistress read one of the longer psalms. The teachers sat with undisguised relief and for once took little or no notice of the girls.

On a few occasions we were permitted to sit—when, for example, dinner tables were assigned on the first day of term or on the historic day that King George VI died. To sit on the floor was always a big relief, but on the day the king died, it was a particular treat, given the long eulogy of the headmistress, who acted like she had lost her father and referred to the dead king, a total stranger to us, as "our beloved monarch." It was not natural to mourn for a man we did not know. Maybe we would have taken King George VI's death more to heart had we known him. Maybe if we had seen his family crying in public, it might have encouraged us to think that he really was someone's father. It's hard to connect at a human level with people who spend most of their lives at charity functions. (I was chatting about the British monarchy recently with a colleague in political science who asked how you can take anyone seriously who wears a tiara. My colleague did not wait for my answer but kept on going: "In America kids dress up in them. But they outgrow them pretty fast.") The most memorable and pleasant aspect of that assembly was that we were all treated like next of kin and given the day off, with the admonition to "go quietly home," advice we duly ignored the minute we hit University Street. Our monarch had died and some of us were going home on the 10:30 bus, to the surprise of Mother in the kitchen.

Assembly, however, was generally not a treat. The King George incident was a historic moment that was not repeated, certainly not by the succeeding monarch, who was ungracious enough to hold her coronation in the summer. All we got out of it was the picnic in Milltown and basking in the reflected glory of a Ballycoan boy who dressed as a mouse and won first prize in the costume contest. However, as far as school holidays were concerned, the House of Windsor contributed nothing to the well-being of the girls of Northern Ireland, unless you were impressed with a summer coronation or monarchical longevity, though the latter may be a more valued commodity in today's Britain than it used to be.

So we plodded on from one assembly to the next, anchored each morning by the hymns in the hymnal called *Songs of Praise,* the Lord's Prayer, and announcements, all delivered in the same monotone voice and with the same amount of zeal. Some hymns should never have been there in the first place, like "Glad that I live am I / That the sky is blue / Glad for the country lanes and the fall of dew." Anyone with a modicum of empathy for those of us who had to walk to the 7:30 bus down these lanes under the gray skies of Ulster would never have penned such a song of praise, unless he or she lived in some bucolic little English village in Shropshire or was simply callous. And then to have to sing it.

But it was not all bleak. On the days when it was Margaret's turn to play the piano, the assembly took on revival tones. Her long fingers could straddle a complete octave, producing sounds from the old piano that raised our tinny voices to new notes of praise and cleared our lungs from the secondhand fumes of Woodbine cigarettes innocently inhaled on the bus on the way to school. The other pianists took no risks, especially with the bottom octaves, and condemned us to singing tunelessly along in spiritless renderings of "Morning has broken like the first morning." After we had recited the Lord's Prayer, the headmistress read from a little prayer book, which contained, as I recall, an inordinate number of "Grant us . . ." The gist of these prayers was that we should all be good, but beyond an occasional allusion to the moral example of Christ and promises of heaven, we were not told how to get there or if it would be worth going to. If a wayward Buddhist had slipped into our midst, she would have been hard pressed to identify the basis of our faith. But as far as I know, parents did not phone the school to complain about or support the religious teachings. If my parents are the gauge, the mild consensus was that the assembly was not doing us much good, but it also was doing us no harm.

Sometimes the headmistress was feeling particularly garrulous and would comment on one of the little generic prayers that she had just read. This invariably caused some furtive eye rolling among the low church girls, who were amused to hear one day that the allusion to hell in the Gospels should certainly not be taken either literally or seriously. It was alright, however, to take the notion of an actual heaven seriously, even though it was mentioned less than hell. Heaven was indeed a destination, and the girls of Princess Gardens were all heading there. Hell did not exist, so the logic went. The cynics among us hoped for her sake that she was right.

While I cheerfully admit that ten years' worth of school assembly and "grant-us" prayers produced feeble returns in my life, my mother's deathbed confronted me some years ago with the Lord's Prayer in a context that I had never encountered. She had always prefaced her every plan with the words "God willing," and now she was dying, and I was losing another reason to return to the province. She would not be in the kitchen or by the fire in her favorite armchair. From the bedroom window I could see the fields shining in May's early morning sun, the cows patiently waiting by the gate to be brought in to be milked. Morning had broken, and nature was apparently going on without me. My mother died as I stood at the window, and the Lord's Prayer was summoned from the depths of my being, not in the way that I had patiently recited it during those ten years at school. Now the words swept over me like a wave, cresting in "Thy will be done on Earth as it is in Heaven," falling again in the quiet recognition that I could bring my gravely human needs in crisis situation to a heavenly father who was not a formula. "Give us this day our daily bread." He would have to take care of tomorrow's bread. There were needs today that I had never met before, a father and brother to comfort and a sister to call home from the United States. My own overwhelming sorrow could only be understood by a heavenly father. My earthly father had temporarily relinquished paternal responsibilities for the role of bereaved husband; he was unable to take care of me and deliver me from "the evil." The presence of death in the hushed room reminded me that my mother had been delivered from all human needs, and it was God's will that she was in heaven. She had settled that issue long before.

I am not sure when it was, but at least two years later the words of an assembly hymn began to reshape in my consciousness, each stanza separated by several weeks. I had not thought of it or heard in all the intervening years. "Lord of all being throned afar / Thy glory shines from sun and star / Center and soul of every sphere / Yet to each loving heart how near." The words were borne along by the memory of Margaret's accompaniment, the bottom octave resonating over the years and miles as majestically as it once filled the school gymnasium, the memory of the vaulting horse still in place, a silent witness to the assembled teachers and girls. "Our midnight is Thy smile withdrawn / Our noontide is Thy gracious dawn / Our rainbow arch Thy mercy's sign / All save the clouds of sin, are Thine." Teachers and girls, prefects, and those they took out of line, even the headmistress, all of us, had experienced firsthand the midnight of withdrawn smiles. Some years ago Miss Crone announced to her aged parents that she was dying. It turned out to be a heart attack. An easy-going, cherished classics teacher was to die in a car crash, and several women, among them my own dear cousin, would experience slow, painful deaths. Some lives may not have been infiltrated by the prayers and hymns of the school assembly, but, then, had they ever been open to the bottom notes when Margaret played?

Was assembly as anemic and innocuous as we once thought? Maybe those harmless little prayers had granted us more protection from hidden dangers over the years than we ever imagined. Perhaps the spiritual returns in my life were not as feeble as I thought. After all, we sang and recited them day after day, repeating stanzas of hymns when the headmistress was late, waiting until the swish of her academic gown finally gave our day permission to proceed. Had we, in fact, invoked a presence that would haunt us like the Hound of Heaven until we finally gave up running?

But what about the fourth stanza? "Lord of all life, below, above / Whose light is truth, whose warmth is love, / Before thy ever-blazing throne / We ask no lustre of our own." I was to find it unexpectedly in the autumn of 1994, sitting in the Memorial Church in Harvard Yard, killing an hour until my daughter came back from class in the Science Center nearby. There it was—"Lord of all being throned afar," written, according to the notes at the end of the hymnal, by Dr. Oliver Wendell Holmes, who had graduated from Harvard when he was twenty.

I later found out that Dr. Holmes was the father of the Supreme Court justice of the same name. Born in Cambridge to a distinguished Boston family, the senior Holmes died at age eighty-five in his home on Beacon Street. Scion of the privileged Brahmin social order, Holmes appears to have found deep joy in the sights that his native city offered: "A man can see further . . . from the top of Boston State House, and see more that is worth seeing, than from all the pyramids and turrets and steeples in all the palaces in the world." As a young man he had studied medicine in Paris, where he had sought out the friendship and companionship of fellow Bostonians. (Maybe he should have spent his time better, perhaps by visiting Villeneuve St. Georges). I read his biography and came up with all sorts of wonderful connections to Margaret's playing the hymn in the gym at Princess Gardens. According to the author Liva Baker, Dr. Holmes's grandmother, Sarah Wendell, apparently found the atmosphere at home too stiff for her liking and dissipated the gloom of the old Calvinist hymns with lilting Irish melodies played on the piano she had imported from London. Surely, she would have approved of the way Margaret added some extra flourishes to the words of Holmes's hymn in a school in Belfast, in as lusterless a room as the mind can imagine.

I also learned that Dr. Holmes did important research on a fever that was striking young mothers, predominantly poor women in Boston, tracing the epidemic to inadequate hospital hygiene, a charge that his colleagues immediately attacked. It was a good thing he wasn't a luster seeker, for it took years before his colleagues finally acknowledged that Holmes's findings were accurate. Reading a biography tends to raise questions about how the next generation turned out, so I kept on going and concluded that other connections, beyond the grandmother's piano, were relevant, like Justice Holmes's dissenting vote in 1923 that struck down state laws prohibiting the teaching of foreign languages to elementary and junior high school students, and the fact that his two closest friends were Jewish jurists. But my favorite readings were from later diaries, when Justice Holmes was getting on in years. Baker writes: "In his later years he delighted in his summer holidays by the sea, renewing his delight in the rocks and ever changing sea and windswept down." Information like that was enough for me to forgive his father for hanging around Bostonians in Paris. But it gets even better, for toward the end of his life Justice Holmes wanted his days "to pass as a rock in the bed of a river, with water flowing over it."

I wonder how far this generation of Harvard students can see. And do they ever worry about acquiring too much luster? But more important, would my own girl with the deep blue eyes of the Wee Wild One get enough sleep in her room in Canaday right under these pealing bells? Surely, it helped some that she went to class wearing the stout black leather shoes that her granddad had bought for her in Lisburn market. And what about her mother? Would the last stanza of Dr. Holmes's hymn ever be answered in her life? "Grant us Thy truth to make us free, / And kindling hearts that burn for Thee / Till all Thy living altars claim / One holy light, one heavenly flame."

9

"When the Cows Go Out
to the Spring Grass"

A frequent guest at our kitchen table was big Willie John Farrow from a farm on "right land" down on the shores of the Lough. That's what my dad called it, as opposed to "oul grass bravely ate down," which he was not beneath calling another man's pastures. Willie John always came right at teatime, as if he had heard the kettle singing and the wheaten farls being lined up alongside the currant scones, Veda bread, and Ormo bakery sponge cake. After eating a hearty tea, in summer a salad that always consisted of the same ingredients—ham, tomatoes, scallions, egg slices, and in later years a peach slice, a culinary addition borrowed from a cousin who moved in high circles—Willie John would settle his large frame into the best chair in the house. It was my dad's favorite, and his barely concealed annoyance did not melt until the conversation landed on the backs of their respective cattle and cow herds. The men's talk revealed as much about language as cattle, though neither was aware at the time of his contribution to their native argot.

As a child I loved to sit in the kitchen and listen to the conversation of others. It was a habit I carried into adult years but with an increasing sense of urgency to transcribe what I had heard into a trusty jotter, yet another tangible connection to my early education. This note-taking had always been part of my frequent pilgrimages from Wisconsin to County Down, but as my dad grew older it became a more pressing activity, as if preserving his words in my blue jotter would keep him with me longer and bind me more closely to the land that he loved so deeply. One day I would transcribe his expressions and stories.

I had the advantage of living for several years in rural Wisconsin, close enough to a dairy farm to be reminded of and reconnected to the daily rhythms of the land as I drove to and from work in the city. The visible routine transmitted a certain comfort that some things in life are fixed—the morning and evening milking, the lighted barn in winter, the smell of silage and dung, the shape of Friesian cows. Yet even an untrained eye would see that the cows in Wisconsin are different from their Irish counterparts: Their routine is shaped far more by the whims of the weather. Irish cows roam around the hills for two-thirds of the year, lying down against the shelter of hedges when the notion comes on them, ambling at their own pace when pursued by a border collie nipping at their heels. The Irish cows have the life of Reilly, compared to their sisters here, who huddle around the barn for three months before disappearing inside without trace for the rest of the year. Then in winter Wisconsin cows frequently slip on ice and break their legs. Their hind quarters have even been known to freeze on desperately cold days.

These are some of the facts that I discovered when my dad made his first and only trip to Wisconsin. I have never seen a human being take a greater interest in rural life than my late father did in Wisconsin. Hail or shine, he draped himself out the open car window just in case he would miss a blade of grass. He plied the farmers with questions, which I translated when the Ulster vernacular got in the way of comprehension. Above all, he wanted to know where the local cattle mart was, how often they sold their cattle, and where they all met to discuss such sales. He could not get over the reply: that some farmers rarely socialize with other farmers, that they have no local cattle mart, never mind a wee cafe at the back of the mart with homemade soup, where farmers in his county—my father pointed out—did more business than at the sales ring. What struck me in the course of these conversations was that the farmers sounded like any other worker in Wisconsin, that their use of language did not set them apart from others in the state. And they looked at my father like he was from another planet. (Maybe they were right.) For it was the way he used the English language that caught their ear, the way he talked about his own and their cows, as if they were fantastic creatures, bestowed on farmers as a special privilege, with a higher purpose than giving milk. And yet his language was fundamentally the same as the one spoken by farmers in the eastern part of County Down. So maybe it is language—the vernacular—that conferred significance upon the cows.

My dad thought that Wisconsin was a powerful place all together. And the beasts (pronounced "bastes") were powerful too. After his death I began to pull together the notes that I had taken in the kitchen of conversations with his farmer friends. In my memory—and notebook—I transcribed the cows of Northern Ireland into two broad categories—quare bastes and middlin' bastes. To the former camp belonged cows with "four tits sitting up the right way," while the others were either "big oul cows with big oul elders [udders] and big oul hind legs" or "wee skelleps [small ugly cows] with no bags on them." I recall that one poor soul was "a third calver [fecund cow] missing a hind tit." It was hard to determine what in fact constituted a "fair bit of a cow," but it was absolutely clear what "a middlin' heifer" was. For one thing, she had no hind feet worth talking about and "oul hair stickin' up on her" and "no belly to her and all up on the legs." Too much hair on her front quarter was a sure sign that she had been covered with salve for dear knows what, and the hair was a dead giveaway. "Och now, man dear," Willie John would always conclude, "You want a maker [good cow] in the ring. Not an oul coat hanger."

It was amazing how much of the conversation was confessional. Each man would cheerfully retrieve the worst judgments on the "bastes" they had bought since the last war. Neither reminded the other that he had already heard the story many times. Their being "had" often involved believing another farmer, like one of "them boys from Downpatrick." You had to be careful with them. Willie John once bought a fair bit of a cow from "that body—Hughie Patterson—and when I got her home and hosed down, sez I, 'Thon's a middlin' heifer.' I was fairly took back. So I was."

These endless conversations between two farmers never drifted far from the sales rings of the province and were dotted with surnames not found in the registers of the local Orange Order. Not that surnames were used. This was first name territory, and Paddy and Seamus popped up in the conversation nearly as often as Willie, Tommy, and Big John. The unifying principle around which this apparently nonsectarian attitude moved on an island of bigotry was nothing less than a correct appraisal and fair treatment of the common cow. A coat hanger was to be treated as a coat hanger by Protestants and Catholics alike, and if you had the misfortune of rearing one, you had better not represent her as a quare baste, regardless of where the man hung his hat on a Sunday. Oul skelleps and middlin' heifers gave you more than a common language beyond the Orange Hall or Hibernian marches. They were the backbone of ethical business deals and determined who would go to your wake.

Big Willie John's story had actually begun much earlier. So let me go back in time to an annual summer excursion to the Strangford Lough. Willie was a bachelor who lived with his bachelor brother Sam and an unmarried older sister, Minnie, in a little community called Ringhaddy on the shores of the Lough. Once a year Minnie rang to invite my parents for tea. "And be sure and bring the weans [wee ones]," she would add in a voice that didn't need phone wires.

We would set off in the green Morris Oxford and head for Comber, then take a side road through Killyreagh that hugged the shore all the way to the Farrows' lane at the side of the Lough. You had to open (and close) two iron gates along their loney, to use the local vernacular for lane, before you pulled up in front of the low single-story whitewashed house overlooking the Strangford Lough. Minnie would be standing outside in her best pinny (a pinafore-style apron), having heard the clank of the last gate. Her white hair was pulled up in a bun, and she would declare each year with the same conviction, "You're as welcome as the flowers in May." And that we were. The parlor smelled of Mansion Polish, the tea table was already set and covered with a kitchen cloth to keep the flies off the plum jam, and Sam was sitting in the corner, dressed in his Sunday best, shining like a mouse. Willie John could scarcely conceal his impatience to get to the real purpose of the visit—to show off his livestock.

My mother had first introduced the Farrows to my father, so her presence on the annual visit to Ringhaddy was more than spousal. My mother had grown up in Ballyhalbert on the other side of the Ards peninsula, the same "Shoreline" that Seamus Heaney so unforgettably described: "Turning a corner, taking a hill / In

County Down, there's the sea / Sidling and settling to the back of a hedge." My mother had known Minnie's family for years. The two women shared the same love for what they called "the tide." To them it was not the shore or the beach or even the sea. It was the tide, and they acted like they had been there when its limits had been set—"thus far and no further." Yet it was this same tide that threw the whole identity of the Farrow farm into question for me. In fact, I still ponder it in the same way as I do Lake Michigan.

I have never been able to warm up to Lake Michigan. They say in Wisconsin that it's just like the sea. Someone once told me that you could submerge England in it. But that's just talk, and nobody has ever tried, even as a possible solution to the so-called Irish question. Lake Michigan remains for some of us a big ostentatious fraud, masquerading as the sea with the odd far-flung wave until caught in winter with its edges frozen solid. But the real reason for my resistance is quite different: Just try mourning your mother along its beaches, and you'll soon find out for yourself how shallow the sound of its waves is. You'll be on the first plane, heading back to the Irish coast and the beach at Portstewart or Port Ballyntrae. So identity remains a serious business, and the question of the Farrow farm is worth pursuing. Can you take a farm seriously that had a hay shed that backed onto the sea? Again, I need Heaney's words—"A tide / is rummaging in / At the foot of all fields." And what about cattle grazing on the island that you could see from the parlor window? The whole thing was ridiculous altogether. For children brought up surrounded by hills, this farm seemed an unlikely place to send the cows out to the spring grass. Maybe we sensed even then that farmland and sea were never meant to put up with each other's smells and moods on a narrow peninsula flanked by saltwater.

I still see the old rowboat tethered to the wall, bobbing up and down on the bloated seaweed that drifted in with the tide and became both plaything and snack to hens—Rhode Island Reds—as they pecked their way daintily along the stony beach. Later, at teatime, Minnie set up a salad with eggs that had bright orange yokes—from the hens eating seaweed. At least that was my mother's explanation. And she ought to know, for the children at Ballyhalbert Elementary School had once teased my uncle Hugh about the color of their hens' egg yokes. "Ma heart was turned," Vida Devoy had said in the broad Scottish dialect of the peninsula. "Oor Sarah's heart was turned," she went on. And she kept on relentlessly with the final insult: "All oor hearts were turned by your eggs." The story stuck in me and I recalled it when I first heard the French expression "J'ai mal au coeur." After all, Ballyhalbert and the fishing port of Portovogie, a few miles around the coast, had their fair share of Huguenots, driven to us after the Troubles in France. But I doubt if little Vida Devoy was thinking about linguistic transliterations when she was struggling to keep down her boiled egg. I also doubt that the present generation with *de*'s in their name are wondering whether their ancestors should have fled somewhere else.

To return to Willie John's farm and the question of its true identity—it would be unjust not to memorialize it as a farm all these years later. For starters, the table talk was as much about the price of heifers as it was farther inland in County Down; even shy Sam would add his assessments of some powerful bastes. And there were other unmistakable signs beyond the open parlor window where cow dung, new hay, and honeysuckle gamely held their ground against the tangy salt air. And there is always the ultimate litmus test for a farm, which can be invoked in extremis—a quiet pee in one of the farm sheds, interrupted at most by the odd cat nonchalantly walking by, apparently used to the sight.

To be frank, the annual visit to Ringhaddy was by no means perfect. Two realities intrude too insistently on my memory to be treated merely as local color: Minnie's mustache and her homemade butter. You could have accepted the mustache if she had confined it to straining her tea, but I, as the youngest in the family—"the child"—had to suffer through a kiss both on arrival and departure, the former making the anticipation of the latter a more dreaded certainty and giving a unique meaning to me of the word *dreadlocks*. The rancid-tasting butter that even the plum jam could not subdue just about wiped out the after tea treats—being rowed by Willie John to one of the islands in the Lough and exploring old ruins in the five acres that turned up years later in an Irish tourist brochure as the remains of a medieval fortress.

It would also be unjust to write about Irish cows and their owners without a culminating celebration of the annual happening that is captured in the title of this story. Broadly speaking, it is the cultural equivalent of transhumance in Provence or the cattle drives in the western part of the United States. Narrowly speaking, it is the equivalent of eating the first new potatoes from Scrabo—before the farmers started bloating them with too much fertilizer—but readers may not be acquainted with those lush fields that skirt the Lough between Comber and Newtownards. It's not like Irish cows hibernate for the whole winter. There are fine days even in January when you could put the cows out. But there comes a day, typically in the middle of March, when showers, sun, and grass conspire in a relationship that produces a sap in the grass, which I suspect was the base for the elixir in the story of Tristan and Isolde. The trouble is that the framework is so beguiling that you could miss the grass. Whins (gorse) inflame the hills from Ballycoan all the way up to Drumbo. Primroses and tiny little violets cling to the shelter of the ditches of the Stable Brae, and bluebells cover Gilliland's glen right down to the river. If you don't like nature, this is not the place for you.

Yet, as lovely as it was and still is, a higher law is at work in mid-March. It is time for the cows to go out to the spring grass. It takes a lot of resistance not to fall under the spell of Ireland in the spring. It could rain for a full fortnight and tourists—especially Americans—still come back raving about everything from the Guinness and the people who drink it to the quaintness of the cows ambling along the narrow roads. Few notice whether those cows are quare beasts or oul skelleps. If the truth were known, few care. But the sad thing is, nobody asks where the cows are going. And even if they knew, would they really care that it was the spring grass? Would they resist its magic, just as some of us can write with a certain detachment about a herd of Wisconsin Friesians as just that—a herd? Or even worse, would they drive with a hard heart along the shore of Lake Michigan, hurling childish insults at its identity?

10

"Where the Mountains of Mourne Sweep Down to the Sea"

There were few sweeter words for us in the English language than "Lord dismiss us with Thy blessing," the hymn that closed the school year and launched the summer holidays. Even though the new term in September would begin with the singing of its twin, "Lord, behold us with Thy blessing, / Once again assembled here," it was such a ridiculously long time in those days from the end of June till the beginning of September that the thought of ever being assembled again anywhere near a school, especially in this same old gym, was simply too remote to even consider. For now it was a time to relish every aspect of leave taking.

We had cleared our desks, and instead of the usual classes we played games with the form mistress, who might even allow the more brazen among us to mimic the teachers. One with a tremendously long neck provided a couple of really cheap laughs, what with her uncanny ability to stretch it out halfway across the room and her boring list of what to lay on the desk before us. "Take out your pencils, your rulers, your jotters, your notebooks," she would drone on every day, as if we kept more exotic things in our bags. There was nothing to take from our bags today and only the tattered remains

of our school term to pack. We treated our table nap-
kins gingerly to prevent a nuclear fallout of mincemeat,
and all that was left of the long term was the final
assembly, ending with a spirited rendering of "Lord
dismiss us." It was now noon, and we were well on our
way to the Mourne Mountains. But not quite, for we
still had to wait for the Twelfth Week.

As I recall, no one in my family or in any other family ever questioned the logic of calling a week that actually fell during the second week of July "the Twelfth
Week," like some massive, culminating event straight
out of the Apocalypse. Of course, as the world knows,
now that our dirty laundry has been hung out overseas,
on July 12 the Orangemen of Northern Ireland parade
in their best suits, bowler hats, and marching shoes to
commemorate the Battle of the Boyne. The world also
knows all about Garvaghy Road and the Ormeau Road
and not just because of Hillary Clinton's wee cup of
tea. (The Garvaghy Road is arguably the most dis-
puted thoroughfare in the province. Situated near the
Protestant-dominated town of Portadown, the road has
been considered by the Orangemen for many generations to be the rightful path for their July march to
Drumcree Church, a site of memory for the Orange
Order. Inhabitants of the same road hold a very different perspective and view the marches as provocation,
especially since violent riots broke out there in 1986.)
The perspective of a child, at least as I recall it, puts a
slightly different spin on the Twelfth. First, it was the

Twelfth Week and not just a one-day march, even if you could see the marchers twice in one day—on their way to the Field, where Orangemen congregate to eat a meal and listen to speeches, and on their way back from the Field. For some people the Twelfth Week was actually the Twelfth Fortnight. I was one of those lucky people.

"Lord dismiss us" was still drying on the gym walls when we set sail to spend two weeks with our bachelor uncles near Newcastle, in a lovely old house with a full view of the Mournes from the window of the bedroom in which our granny had died when I was an infant. Other girls went with their parents to Groomsport for a month in a rented house or a caravan, or to the Kildara Lodge in Portrush for a week, but we went to our uncles. And we went without parents. We did not need parents in the place we were spending our holidays. Our uncles were elderly, had always been so, and were hard of hearing and shortsighted. They were not Orangemen, did not own marching shoes, and had never seen a Twelfth parade in their lives. Their only connection to the annual event was our visit, which interrupted a life that otherwise revolved around their garden, a large wireless set on the kitchen shelf, and Sunday lamb dinner with their other bachelor brother. Each year they expected us for the Twelfth Fortnight, complete with a brown hard-backed case that contained among our clean clothes a large container of Nivea Cream, which was supposed to attract the sun. Both men were considered quite eccentric by the rest of the family—frankly, the word *odd* was used—but to us they were an answer to prayer, in that we could come and go when we liked. Admittedly, the three steps at the top of the staircase creaked so loudly that we had to perform the splits to avoid hitting them at midnight, but this was altogether a treat and a half for three children aged ten to fourteen.

Newcastle was a den of iniquity, at least to those of us who did not know much about dens. Home to a troupe of Pierrots with southern Irish accents and dissipated faces, the town also offered an amusement arcade with dodgems and slot machines, where pennies teetered at the edge of a great mound of coins, literally poised to fall into your hand, provided you kept feeding the machine. Mysteriously, nothing budged. We had saved our bus money by thumbing a lift into town, so we were able to spend our allowance on something useful like the slot machines. From dawn to dusk (which didn't fall till well into the night) the Twelfth Fortnight was a great carry-on. Our uncles' maid came each morning at nine and made breakfast for the uncles and reluctantly for us. You could tell from the dour look on her face that the Twelfth fortnight was not her idea of a holiday. She was a Catholic, so no wonder.

One gesture was required on our part to ensure that the annual holiday was kept in perpetuity—a daily walk around the garden with the older uncle, who spoke for both of them. The purpose of the walk was twofold: to view the roses and to admire the way that he had memorized their names in Latin. His face took

on a beatific glow when he pronounced names that fell
from his lips like balm. The garden was a complete
wilderness, as neither of my uncles was given to hard
manual work or the whole notion of aesthetic order.
While they had done moderate work as younger men,
they certainly would never be mentioned in a manual
for the promotion of the work ethic. They simply liked
roses, and they didn't care if the roses were buried
among weeds, gooseberry bushes, raspberry canes,
plum trees, and nettles. They would order by mail the
most exotic roses from all over the United Kingdom
and proceed to plant them in the middle of the densest
undergrowth in the garden. Oddly enough, the roses
thrived among the weeds. A large concrete tank right
under our bedroom window collected the rainwater
that our uncles used to water all these brilliant flowers,
which flourished behind the shelter of a thick spruce
hedge, well out of sight from the rest of the world. The
older uncle always referred to every flower in the world
by its Latin name, even the foxglove, which he transformed into a *Digitalis purpurea,* and a harmless wee
daisy got a double-barreled name—*Chrysanthemum
leucanthemum.* He knew I was learning Latin and in-
correctly presumed my interest. I didn't give a rip.

The younger uncle rarely said a word in any language and looked happiest when he was attending to
his sweet pea in the smaller front garden. In fact, he
may have been silently protesting his older brother's
Latin-dominated chaos at the back, for his little front

lot was carefully kept, the sweet pea meticulously braced on a sturdy fence. The subtle pastel colors and sweet fragrance of the sweet pea might have been an inviting entrance to the house, if anyone had ever visited them. We always arrived at the back door and made our way through the scullery to the living room, where the older uncle, already going blind from glaucoma that was diagnosed too late to help him, awaited our arrival. It was actually our mother's voice that cheered him, for he knew that her shopping bag always brought treats that he never knew existed.

On the first day of our holiday we would set off mid-morning for a dip in the tide, that is, if the weather were half-decent. This entailed walking through high sand dunes studded with flowers that could have kept my uncle in business for life. But he never left his own garden. Dramatic as any hill you have ever seen in a Hollywood western—if you were allowed to go to the pictures—these sweeping dunes drew all sorts of wild possibilities from our childish fantasies. You could imagine just about anything in the struggle against the driving wind—handsome cowboys with an American accent riding out of nowhere, rescuing us from sandstorms. When we finally reached the sea, there wasn't a soul in sight all the way along the deserted beach; the Slieve Donard Hotel away in the distance was the first indicator that we were near a major resort. But the day was long, and we had two full weeks of freedom and not just any old weeks but the Twelfth Fortnight when the world paraded along Newcastle Strand. This was the perfect start to the day—the adventure of the dunes, the dip in the sea, and then biscuits and lemonade.

The reason I have never learned to swim can be traced to these mornings along the dunes near the Twelve Arches, between Dundrum and Newcastle. I submit that any person who frequented these beaches as a child never learned to swim anywhere. The trick was to get in and out of the water again as quickly and as safely as possible. Even in July the water temperature was never known to be above freezing. When I see cowardly people race out of Lake Michigan in the middle of summer, my sense of derision knows no bounds, especially when I consider that they are not fleeing from jellyfish. We would dip in and out several times, returning to the shelter of the dunes to dry off and simply enjoy the sight of the Irish Sea tossing and turning up and down the beach for our personal amusement. Later, when I read Thomas Mann's *Tonio Kröger,* I wondered why young Tonio got his knickers in such a twist by envying boring old Hans Hansen's swimming in the Baltic Sea, when all Tonio could do was watch it. Thomas Mann should have come with us for a quick dip in the tide near Newcastle, and he would have soon agreed that seas are meant to be looked at first and foremost, frequently dipped in, at times cried at, but they don't have to be swum in to prove a thing about you. Certainly, they should never be used to fob off such a bipolar identity on characters.

But of course in those days we were not thinking about Thomas Mann or any other Germans—whether willing or unwilling executioners—for the next level of our day was about to be entered, namely, the walk toward Newcastle in the hope of a lift—a free ride from a passing motorist. We were rarely disappointed. The beach at Newcastle held little interest for us and on the rare warm day was filled with mothers and children playing with buckets and spades. We were well beyond the bucket-and-spade stage and in fact had never been attracted to either. Our interest lay beyond the wall that separated the main street called the Strand from the esplanade. The pier at Newcastle was actually at the other end of the town and was in fact not the hub of the resort, as is the case in many British seaside resorts. The center of activity here was a grassy area with a couple of beds laid out with solid working-class flowers like snapdragons and marigolds and flanked on each side by a paved walk with wooden benches. Thus life moved on three tiers, the highest of which was the street level, jammed with cars and drivers looking for a parking spot; the esplanade level with two major activities (to be explained presently); and the beach level or the bucket-and-spade level. Low walls divided these three areas but only in the physical sense, for many people came to Newcastle for the express purpose of sitting on a wall. Nobody thought it strange to go for a holiday on a wall, and in fact, when my American husband, on his first visit to Newcastle, commented on this phenomenon, I recognized with a start that I had married a man who would have to learn from scratch the art of sitting on a wall on a Saturday evening.

The top level had some appeal to us, in that the little café attracted interesting people, like ourselves and soldiers with odd English accents from Ballykinlar army camp. The cafe was roughly the equivalent of rural Wisconsin diners, like Blondie's in Oconomowoc and Norske Nook, way up north in the state, which have genuine plastic flowers and serve homemade pecan rolls and beer-battered fish fries every Friday night. (It is a shame that they get so little notice in the Best Dining section of the newspaper.) In Newcastle we sampled the local dishes—plaice and chips, sausages and chips, and toward the end of the fortnight beans on toast, always accompanied by a pot of tea and wheaten scones and jam. It was gourmet living at its best.

Newcastle's heart was on the next level where the Pierrots—street actors, really—performed three times daily. The last show of the evening, however, was by far and away the best, for they had saved their most exciting tricks for people too weary or impaired by the local beverage to question the validity of their magic. A piano player banged away on an old upright and doubled as a magician. He would wander among the audience, holding up sundry items to his colleague, blindfolded on the stage, who would triumphantly announce that he was holding the expired driving license of Thomas F. Scott or the Ponds lipstick of a woman from

Rathfriland. It was magic altogether and we were the first to applaud. We would have applauded louder had it not been for the presence of preachers of the gospel, who occupied the other half of the esplanade. Troubling hymns like "Where will you spend eternity?" rose in the tangy air, mingling with the jangle of the piano on stage and the jingle of the collection can that the Pierrots shook right in your face. Besides, it was late and no matter how deaf your uncle was, it was high time to head for the road. A little cottage with "Shell Haven" on the gate was the halfway point between Newcastle and the Twelve Arches, accurately calculated by three weary children; thumbing a lift at night was one of the few risks that we did not take. So we pattered on, taking the optimistic view that "Shell Haven" meant we were halfway home.

The Twelfth Fortnight ended for us the day our dad's blue Morris Oxford drove into the uncles' backyard. We had not seen a single Orangeman the whole time. Our bathing costumes were retrieved from the clothesline, looking for all the world like the tattered remnants of an umbrella. The brown hard-backed case was poised for home, complete with pink and white rock bearing the inscription "Greetings from Newcastle." My mother never looked more like a mother. To tell you the truth, "Shell Haven" had been shifting for me and was nowhere near the halfway point between Newcastle and the Twelve Arches. Increasingly, there were quarrels among us on the nightly walk home.

Mention was made more than once that I was a baby, with the adjective *big* thrown in to make the road even longer. There were uncalled-for references to the tell-tale egg yoke down my front. Apparently, I could be taken nowhere, either before or after dark. The culminating insult came one evening when my sister told me that I was a nuisance. The attractive boy lurking in the shadows had wanted to walk her home. And Newcastle itself was quickly losing some of its allure. In certain light the mountains of Mourne could look positively sinister sweeping down to the sea. Our pocket money long since gone, we were no longer impressed with the Free State accent of the Pierrots when they shook their money tin under our face. Where we spent eternity might indeed be worth exploring. The Pierrots began to look as tired as I felt. The presence of the farmers and their wives sitting along the walls, gaping at other tired farmers and their wives who were looking for a free spot to sit, underscored the pervasive fatigue that had fallen over the Twelfth. If this fortnight didn't end soon, some of us would have to stay at home and join the marches or, even worse, end up making sand castles on the beach level, playing with a bucket and spade, along with the other big babies.

11

Quare Craic

The most conducive venues for good *craic* in Northern Ireland used to be the bus and the local bridge, two modes of communication that came together in a powerful nexus when the bus stop happened to be located at the side of the bridge. This was the case at the Leverogue, the townland that borders Ballycoan, and at Purdysburn bridge, but in the latter case the *craic* was electrified by the arrival of the last bus from town on a Saturday night, when nurses and parlor maids who worked and lived at Purdysburn Fever Hospital alighted in full view of a dozen or so young men, among them three who were semipermanent fixtures at the bridge— Geordie Chisholm, Bertie Boyd, and Alex Bruno.

The No. 13 bus kept on going up to the Leverogue (the definite article always accompanies the Leverogue), but the bridge up there was less of a magnet because there was not a hospital or a nurse in sight, so the area was totally dependent on local talent, confined at the time to a cluster of houses near the bridge that harbored singularly unremarkable people. (That too, of course, could have changed in the last thirty years.) There was, however, a credible river at the Leverogue, with its own personal waterfall called the Gray Mare's

Tail, which compensated in natural beauty for what the area lacked in good *craic*. In short, it was not a place you would ever choose to alight from a bus, unless you wanted to catch spricks (tiny fish) at the foot of the Gray Mare's Tail. We often did as children, but since we approached the waterfall from another direction, wading upstream in our Wellington boots all the way from Gilliland's glen, we really could not have seen how many people got off the bus at Leverogue corner with empty bottles for spricks. Besides, we were too immersed in the adventure of our favorite local excursion to notice anything other than the fun we were having—taking off our Wellingtons to ensnare the spricks, pushing one another in and out of the water, checking out the hazelnut trees for signs of a good harvest that we would later cull. It was *quare craic*.

It is time, however, to return to the hub of social life in Purdysburn, where the bus is due any minute now. It had left Ormeau Avenue at 10:45 on the dot, had picked up more people along the Dublin Road, among them Stan Nugent, at least on the day he had won a few quid on the horses. Stan loved to have a flutter on the horses and often squandered his week's wages at Barney Eastwood's betting shop. The story goes that one day Stan actually had enough gall to complain to Barney Eastwood that he had bet away the week's wages and that he didn't have a shilling to give to the missus to feed the weans. Stan then showed Barney the dangling sole of his shoe, adding that he had nothing left to buy the groceries. Barney was supposed to have taken from his inside pocket a big wad of bank notes held together by a thick elastic band, which he carefully removed, before handing it to Stan with the words, "Wrap that 'round your shoe. It'll get you home."

Stan never did give up the horses and was a regular on the 10:45, boarding at the end of the Dublin Road. The bus would then proceed with Stan past Shaftesbury Square, up Bradbury Place, to the stop in front of the Crescent Church, where it picked up people who had been at the "Help Heavenward" meeting, then on to Queens University for a few local students who had gone to the weekly hop, then pulled in at the last stop of the journey, right in front of the Eglantine Pub, where two women — known as the Hardy Annuals — could barely stagger on board. From there it was a clear ride home all the way up the Malone Road, past bus stops where not a soul was waiting for the No. 13 bus, for why would people from such a fashionable road choose to take the last bus on a Saturday night to Purdysburn or the Leverogue, even if they knew that local folklore was being spun at that very hour on the bridge at the foot of Purdysburn Hill?

Not that the *craic* was bad before the bus arrived. In fact, on some nights it was the best part of the evening. Like the night Mr. Oakwood, who lived up the Ballycoan road beyond John Moore's corner house — the one with the high hawthorn hedge that had just been trimmed — delivered his locally famous rebuke to

Geordie Chisholm. Mr. Oakwood was well named, for he was an out-and-out vegetarian at a time when every man, woman, and child in the townland was eating bacon and sausage for breakfast, lamb or pork chops for dinner, cold ham sandwiches for tea, and possibly a mixed grill or Ulster fry as a snack before going to bed. And if you couldn't afford the food groups represented in this pyramid, there was always a good lard sandwich. These early eating habits may indeed have contributed in some way to the high rate of heart disease in the province, but mortality rates have probably also been mitigated by other factors, like low stress levels found on or near bridges and the inordinate helpings of orange and green vegetables that accompanied the meat.

On this particular evening Mr. Oakwood was his usual polite self. "Goodnight, gentlemen," he said poshly, for he was from the south of England and had resisted the vernacular of his adopted country. "Goodnight, Mister Oakwood," Geordie answered in the same tone of voice—a perfect imitation—down to the final crisp dental. Mr. Oakwood stopped dead in his tracks, wheeled around in the middle of the bridge, and delivered as eloquent a speech on the benefits of a British education as you would hear in a day's travel. These young men, lounging casually at various angles on the bridge or the handlebars of their bikes, were informed that the British government was spending a fortune in the province to combat ignorance such as Geordie had just displayed. The Ministry of Education was offering these young hooligans the same high level of learning found all over the United Kingdom. And what was the outcome? His eloquence increased in direct proportion to the implied futility of spending English money on educating the North Irish. The whole project was beginning to look like a colossal flop, thanks to Geordie Chisholm's imitation of Mr. Oakwood's accent, which was so good, so imbued with moral failure, that it was about to bring down the government.

Mr. Oakwood continued crisply on his way toward Milltown, but the "gentlemen" were not at all put out by the lecture and carried on like the British government's investment in their lives had been worth every farthing. They also knew that they could depend on Geordie's wit to think up something for the encounter with Mr. Oakwood when he walked back home from Milltown, still fresh as paint from a lifetime of good eating and walking habits. But the bus was just turning the sharp corner farther up the road, and already the nurses and maids were standing up and straphanging their way to the back of the bus, past the Hardy Annuals, who were perched on the side seat, for frankly that's about as far as their legs would carry them when they boarded at the Eglantine.

Some parenthetical comments are clearly in order at this point, to provide readers with visual aids to the people who regularly traveled on the No. 13 bus. I am, of course, not referring to the early-morning 7:30 bus, which catered to a very different clientele, most of whom were your average punters—clerical workers in government offices, like the Northern Ireland Housing Trust, women who worked in fruit and vegetable shops on the Lisburn Road or in the millinery department of Robinson and Cleaver's or in Hogg's china shop. Not that this assortment of people was without idiosyncrasies. One younger woman who boarded the bus in front of Downey's shop in Milltown village was the most exotic looking woman outside Spain. Everybody looked at her because she was so gorgeous, with an olive complexion, huge brown eyes, and long dark hair. People said that she had to be foreign, for she was far too good-looking to be from around our way, especially if she happened to sit beside the woman who got on near Shaw's Bridge. The contrast between the two women was spectacular. The Shaw's Bridge woman had watery pale blue eyes and had plastered on her face an inch of thick white powder that clung in big chunks to her eyelashes, like cement on a mixer. She was a sketch. Interspersed among the travelers on the early bus were schoolchildren in the various uniforms of the city schools—navy and white for Methodist College, dark red for Victoria College, black and yellow for Belfast Academic Institution, and brown and fawn for Princess Gardens. Girls were expected to wear their school beret, boys their school caps, while waiting for the bus and while on board. If caught bare-headed by the Latin teacher, you were liable to incur a punishment of writing in Latin fifty times the transliterated sentence "I must wear my helmet while waiting for the chariot."

In terms of clientele and *craic* the Saturday night 10:45 bus was not the daily 7:30, so there is little point in continuing with these drab descriptions of people like the cement-mixer woman, or Florrie McQuillan, who got on the bus at my stop every morning with her wee brown boring bag and asked even more boring questions—like what you were going to be when you grew up, as if you had any intention of ever doing anything other than observing people on buses, and if she would just move to another seat you could overhear what Johnny Wilton was saying in the backseat, for he was far more entertaining than boring old Florrie. Johnny was en route to spend the day at R. J. Allam's sale yard, but in actuality he would spend most of it in a pub in May Street. Everybody on the bus knew that. All the smokers were lined up on the backseat, Johnny among them, holding forth without the influence of the drink that would later give even more flavor to his talk on the four o'clock bus that took us all home for tea, at least when we didn't get detention after science. I liked Johnny, for he had known my family for years and connected me right there on the No. 13 bus with great grandparents and relatives that I knew only from pictures on the walls. For that alone I liked to sit in the three-person seat right in front of the rear seat and hear his stories about what a fine man my grandfather was. It didn't make any difference to me that he repeated himself and slurred, for I still liked him, even if some people sitting on the two side seats would scowl when he leaned too heavily on his thorn stick and nearly toppled over (couped, we say), especially when he was taking aim with a tobacco-laced spitball, right before the conductor closed the door of the bus. He had perfected the trajectory to an art.

But this is getting far too interesting for daytime, so we better get off the four o'clock and back onto the 10:45 or we'll miss the *craic* with the Hardy Annuals. They were a mother-daughter team, the mother looking like a jaded version of an American movie star of the fifties, with straggly strawberry blond hair that had been subjected to an unsuccessful perm. There is no point describing the daughter, for she was a younger carbon copy of the mother. Both women wore colorful outfits with patterns like screen savers and boldly décolleté blouses that exposed the following week's washing. The mother teetered on and off the bus in high-heeled patent leather shoes, offset with nylons that had butterflies embroidered all the way up her ankle. It is easy to provide these details, for my brother—a consummate observer—saw them with his own two eyes, both women sprawled all over the side seat, looking like they were begging to be written about, even if both would be long since gone by the time they finally appeared in print.

In absolute fairness to both women, they were exemplary neighbors the rest of the time, gave a couple of bob to veterans on Flag Day, helped local farmers get their bullocks back into the field if the animals broke out, and spoke like the rest of us six days a week. The daughter was occasionally seen—and heard—at a monthly dance in Ballycoan Orange Hall, where she loved to be asked to sing. The emcee would announce, "We'll now call on Sadie for her pleasure." One night Sadie started singing "Softly, softly turn the key and open up my heart" on too high a note, and Sammy McDowell was insensitive enough to yell, "Her silencer is gone!" Even worse, he repeated the story at our kitchen table to the farm laborers, within the hearing of a certain young one who hung around the kitchen for more than food.

Drink can do desperate things to a person, and the Hardy Annuals were no exception. In their case it made them religious with an English accent. I would doubt that either had ever taken the night crossing from Belfast to Heysham or Liverpool, but they didn't need to, at least not to acquire an accent, for the Eglantine was a lot nearer home. It was good *craic* the night they landed in on Willie and Artie Patterson, elderly bachelors who farmed a really small holding up in the hills with another equally single older brother, who was rarely seen in public, least of all on a bus. The other two brothers liked to go to Gresham Street on a Saturday evening and hang around the secondhand shops, which sold everything from gramophone records to canaries.

On this particular night on the 10:45 bus, another big farmer, who went by the name of Scallion John, asked them, in a voice loud enough for the driver in the enclosed cab to hear, how the castrating of their pigs had gone the previous Sunday. The question had roughly the same impact as Martin Luther's nailing of the ninety-nine theses to the door of Wittenberg Cathedral. The mother Hardy Annual launched into an eloquent defense of the sabbath, as she called it, and vilified these two men for having profaned it in such a savage way. Had they no shame? The mother's eyes were rolling toward the back of her head at the thought of the carnage. Why were they not at their place of worship on the sabbath? They were able to go to Smithfield's on a Saturday night but not to church. Meanwhile, the daughter had joined in, and their combined accents had taken on shades of every shire in England. The consonant changes and vowel mutations of the Second Sound Shift had nothing on this. The mother was going to report the discussion of pig castration to the minister of the Church of Ireland the very next morning, when she and her daughter would be out of bed in time for the service, she emphasized. The minister would certainly put a stop to such activities in a townland as religious as ours, one that could boast of a distinguished history of sabbath keeping.

The two brothers were visibly shaken by the attack and stared meekly from under their duncher caps at the two women, who by now were positively aglow from vodka and zeal. Every neck all the way up the bus was turned to hear the sermon, and the backseat lads, who were usually the ones to provide Saturday night entertainment on the way home, were hanging on their every word, egging the women on under the influence of their own night out. It was a good thing for the Patterson brothers that the Hardy Annuals were getting off soon, for their own stop was way up in the hills, near the end of the bus line.

But the nurses and parlor maids have been strap-hanging long enough, and it is high time to bring the last bus in, before we forget that the incorrigible hooligans are waiting for us on the bridge. Besides, it has turned cold, and night has fallen far too quickly for a mid-June evening that should still be showing at least a slice of the sinking sun. Bertie thinks he is speaking for all of them when he says, draped over the handlebars of his bike, "I'm founderin'. I wish the bus would come, so that I can get away on home." But he is not speaking for Geordie Chisholm, who has finally spotted Mr. Oakwood on his way back from Milltown, approaching the bridge a matter of minutes behind the bus. Meanwhile, the bus has unloaded the nurses and parlor maids, who have been whistled at half-heartedly by the lads up the hill toward the main gate of the hospital. Geordie has the look of a man with a mission. "Mr. Oakwood," says he, as polite as your boot, when the Englishman was about halfway over the bridge. You could tell by Mr. Oakwood's face that he was poised for an abject apology. "The police are looking for you." The spry vegetarian was clearly taken aback, but not as much as the other fellows on the bridge, who inched their bikes a bit closer to Geordie's to hear what on

Earth their mate had been hatching. "Did they say why?" Mr. Oakwood asked with undisguised agitation. "For eating the tops of John Moore's hedge," Geordie answered clearly, in his own accent, but with the confidence of an Ulsterman on whom the British government's money had been well spent.

12
Hard Men

The hardest man I ever encountered was a woman—a direct ancestor—but I know her only from a large photograph in a black frame that stared down at me uncompromisingly from the dining room wall. They say that when her son got polio as a child, she stayed up for two days and nights without a wink of sleep and rubbed his legs back to life. She also carried another sick child all the way to Purdysburn Fever Hospital in a lace shawl. It turned out to be scarlet fever and he recovered. During the bad flu epidemic in 1918 she bought a black herbal medicine from a homeopathic shop way up the Shankhill, and none of her family contracted the illness, though three members of a local family died of it and were buried on the same day. In that family a sister by the name of Margaret survived, but she was never the same, and in fact people blamed the bad flu of 1918 on every word that the poor woman subsequently said. One evening Margaret was watching a cowboy film along with a neighbor, and during the commercial break she said it was a good thing the horses could get a wee rest when the Persil ads were on. It's a shame that Margaret's mother didn't give her the black herbal medicine that my ancestor doled out to her family, for then she would have noticed that the horses weren't even real. But, then, my grandmother was a hard man. So she was.

Within the mythology of the hard men of Northern Ireland, certain names have entered the canon and are familiar to anyone even vaguely interested in the psychology of hard men. As in other cultures, such as that of the United States, hard men tend to be associated either with large cities like Chicago or with the West, which is outdoors (if ever there was a place that was outdoors). Northern Ireland is no exception, but its capital city is like no other on the face of the earth, because Belfast has been inordinately influenced and infused by the outdoors. Sadly, international cameras have missed this, have focused only on two streets, and elided the rest of its identity, neglecting to inform the world that there is more to Belfast than violence and that Belfast had hard men long before the Troubles.

The trouble with the Troubles is that Hollywood cashed in on what they think are North Irish hard men, dressed them up in leather jackets, taught them how to lower their vowels and drop dental and plosive sounds, washed and actually sprayed their hair, smeared dark powder under their eyes to make them look even harder, and fobbed this construct off on the world. It's a shame. So it is. The protagonist is usually Catholic and the antagonist the British Army. Hard men do not end up in Hollywood. They are lucky if they get as far as the Holwood in County Down. Hard men stay at home, too often the pawns of men who provide the material for Hollywood films. Nationalists are not the only hard men in the province. Hard men cut right across the sectarian divide and among them are the men who paid with their lives in the Maze Prison and who, even after the peace accord, are now struggling on the outside.

Let me suggest certain criteria that have always obtained for the collective identity of hard men: to a wo/man they have been exposed at a frightening level to the vicissitudes of life, they know the back streets of Belfast, have practiced solidarity at its most solid in the Maze, or spent twelve years too long in a mental asylum. Another criterion for hardness is so obvious that I hesitate to even mention it—being scared of your mother. That's what they say, for example, about Silver McKee from the Markets area of Belfast, a place that would instill respect for anybody's mother. At least it used to, before they gentrified the area. I have struggled with the inclusion of Buck Alex in the canon of North Irish Hard Men, not only because he emigrated from the province in the twenties and therefore has lost—like myself—credibility. But he did come back to the province and died in it, which should have some weight, and there is, frankly, *un certain je ne sais quoi* about a man with a shamrock tattoo on his arm, the rumor that he used to be Al Capone's minder, and, above all, that he kept a lion in his backyard in York Street. I confess to being impressed with the latter claim but reject him on the grounds of connection to crime, even though there may not be a word of truth to the rumor. All hard men know and respect one another, like the way Stormy Weatherall from up the Shankhill is said to have respected Silver McKee. The beauty of the reputation of being a hard man is that you can live off your name until you die. They say that Buck Alex did, but, then, I don't even accept him as a hard man.

With that issue settled we can now forge ahead and take an unapproved road into Belfast, the city that has shaped these hard men, the city with unique connections to the farmland that no city north or south of the border can boast of. As you may know, until recently Belfast had a sale yard called Allams within spitting distance of the city center, one that united town and country on a daily basis—beef sales one day, dairy cows the next, sheep, and so on. Every North Irish animal with fur and legs had a day excursion to Belfast. Mind you, for some it was their last day stepping out anywhere, but my point is simple—city people actually saw farm animals. (I am reminded of an incident on a bus in Switzerland when an Englishwoman spotted cows and carried on like she was watching the animals emerge from the ark on Mount Ararat. The North Irishwoman who overheard this outburst later offered it to me as solid anecdotal evidence that English tourists are an embarrassment abroad.)

In this city-country symbiosis that I was attempting to describe, there was little time for violence or the pursuit of sectarian issues, what with hundreds of cattle, cows, and sheep dashing about within blocks of the city hall. The result was that farmers and drovers ended up in a mutual dependence that leveled and lowered both flags. Even children got in on the act and earned a bob or two looking out for parked Land Rovers and other vehicles parked around the market area. The drovers came from the streets of the predominantly Catholic area around the mart (called the Market Area), were able to earn a decent living, and established lasting ties with the farmers—Catholic and Protestant alike from a thirty-mile radius around Belfast. Silver McKee was among the better-known ones. They say he was as hard a man as you could wish to meet. Now try to tell me that he was not from the country.

But we must press on beyond the end of the tram lines and show that the fields around Belfast have always been controlled by animals rather than people. Try applying for a permit to build a house or even a hen house, and you'll soon see how green the belt is. Ordinary, nonfamous people live out there. They live there only if their ancestors claimed the land during the Plantation of Protestants in the seventeenth century or if an old aunt left no will and the house was sold to strangers. Occasionally, some of the strangers act like they are famous, like the woman who told the farmer's wife to stop hanging out her knickers on the clothesline that overlooked the Ballycoan Road—a clothesline that probably predates the crossing of the Boyne.

Very rich people like stars and singers choose to live near Dublin rather than Belfast in stunning settings with hills and the like that are considered—and quite rightly—beautiful. These gorgeous houses, devoid of clotheslines in the vales of Wicklow, are property—prime property—rather than a green belt or ground to fatten your cattle on to send to one of the Dublin marts. The reason these famous people (some of whom maybe even grew up on Belfast streets) chose to live in the hills around Dublin is far more basic than not wanting to get shot at for marrying a Catholic or a Protestant. They do not think that Belfast and environs are beautiful. In a sense they are right—not because the Ballycoan hills are ugly but because Belfast has had such miserable publicity.

Tell people often and persuasively enough that a place is interesting or beautiful or is "a field of dreams," and they will come. I am obviously not suggesting that bus tours should now take in the view of clotheslines on the Ballycoan Road as part of the excursions they offer these days—up the Falls and down the Shankhill, with discreet stops outside the local cemeteries where the nationalist and loyalist "heroes" lie at rest.

But Belfast has had desperate publicity from what President Bush the Elder might have called "the violence thing." It has destroyed the town-country, Protestant-Catholic symbiosis with the closure of Belfast's cattle mart, has not bothered to introduce its other streets, and only recently the city fathers acknowledged that the shores of Belfast Lough were not the only banks it was built on. Local architects designed a splendid concert hall on the banks of the Lagan. Exiles came home to sing and dance in the completed building, which overlooks as neglected a stretch of water as lies east of the Mississippi. All it took was Jimmy Galway and Barry Douglas playing "Danny Boy" (which occasionally functions as our national anthem), and the eyes of the world finally saw the Lagan flowing by like it always did, plus or minus the odd mattress but now spruced up to bask in the reflected glory of the famous exiles singing inside.

The two men I want to write about—after a long warm-up—are not just names in the register of hard men but men I have known. The backdrop of their lives could not be further removed from my uncles' secluded garden behind the spruce hedge near the Twelve Arches, where two soft men shuffled among the roses and weeds. Like my uncles, however, these men are not famous, except to me, and have never sung in the Waterfront Hall, although one of them went to a boxing match there last spring. They respect Jimmy Galway for one reason—he plays the right instrument. (If he ever took up the oboe, he could hang up his career.) Each of them—mentioned or described—has taken a hiding (they say "batin'" in Belfast) in their personal lives, have been captivated once too often by the liquor and/or intoxicating rhetoric of loyalist pubs in East Belfast or Lisburn, and were not as afraid of their mothers (or wives) as they should have been. Both were christened William and were known from childhood on as Billy.

William of Orange could not possibly have antici-
pated that people in the Ireland of his day would take
his name (or his horse) so seriously. A sociologist
should analyze the number of "Williams" registered
since 1690 and plot a topographical map showing
where the largest clusters fall and at what period in history. The analysis should also include "William" as a
middle name, as in "Samuel William," a further reflec-
tor, though clearly more cowardly, of sectarian loyalty.

The first Billy I ever met was, like the people who
lived in Purdysburn village, permanently old. He
looked to me exactly like the picture of my grandfather
on the dining room wall, probably because he was and
remains the only grandfather I have ever known. He
had a thin face with bushy eyebrows, a twinkle in his
eyes reserved exclusively for us children, and a look that
communicated that nothing was a bother to him as
far as we were concerned. If he was working near the
house, you could follow him around the yard or the
fields nearby for hours and feel his protection over you
and his interest in every word you uttered. We quar-
reled to have the chair closest to Billy, who sat at the
head of the table like the patriarch of the family. Yet
Billy's position in our family was the same one that
Sam Harrison had occupied a generation earlier.
Though he was a hard man—and I'll tell why in a
minute—he answered all our questions about life with
the simple response, "You'll have to find all them
things out." And he was right. When he told us there

were no ghosts in the graveyard on Ballycairn Hill, we believed him and quit running our legs off for fear the ghosts would catch up with us and drag us back to their resting place. When the first jet planes started to fly over the province, I remember asking Billy why they made such a terrible noise. "Thon oul planes are all roosted up" was his measured response. A plane that had rusted out was not all that far off the mark. No child in any country could have had a better grandfather than I had in Billy. Every Sunday night he returned from Belfast on the early evening bus with sweets in his pocket for "the weans." We "weans" acted every week like we had never seen such treats in a bag— eyeball sweets, licorice, dolly mixtures, Rowantree's fruit gums. I pity the child who has not run along a lane on a Saturday evening to meet her or his grandfather as he got off the bus with a bag of sweets in his pocket.

I don't know whether Billy had a childhood, but what little he had was spent in the streets off the Donegal Road, near the area referred to as the Village, which had a brief respite during the year of peace when Catholic students from Queens University actually were able to rent flats in the virulently loyalist area, until the peace measures failed and they found notices on their doors telling them to get out or they would be kneecapped. I know that Billy played by the side of the Blackstaff River, for I once overheard him talk about a fight in his youth and about clodding stones at fellows on the other side of the Blackie. They were calling one another Fenian and Orange miscreants, except they used different words. Billy never used much language, including the bad kind, on us, so it would be wrong to use the actual words, for he wasn't talking to me at all.

Billy had spent twelve years in an asylum for the mentally deranged, but he wasn't deranged at all. He had been committed by his wife, who said he had been so drunk that he had torn up the house. When Billy's son came of age, he signed the form to release his father. I am not sure how Billy came to be with us. All I know is that he was the grandfather I never had and that he lived up the lane in the little cottage that belonged to our family, where Sam Harrison died. Billy worked like he was making up for every lost hour of his life and in the evening smoked his pipe in a big red stuffed chair, knocking out the ashes on the open hearth. In his later years, when he was too feeble to work, my mother carried up all his meals, and he still loved to have a cup of tea beside the fire and a pull on his pipe.

As a child I never knew about the long hiatus in Billy's life. Why would you ever suspect that a man who never said a harsh word to you and brought you sweets every Sunday and lit your living room fire and kitchen stove every morning had been locked up for all those years? Among all the farm laborers who worked on our land, no one commanded greater respect than Billy. His physical stamina was extraordinary for a lean, light man. During potato harvest, when workers were brought out on the trailer of the tractor from the toughest and roughest streets of Belfast, it was Billy who kept order among them, working alongside men from both the Falls and the Shankhill. None of them ever squared up to Billy. At threshing time every farmer in the townland knew that Billy's place was at the head of the table. Yet he said little, moving through his daily chores with the steady gait of a man with a purpose, bending now and again to listen to another question of one of the three "weans" who vied for his attention, devoted to the gentle woman who had, on the death of my grandmother, become mistress of the house, the title that he always used to address her. He was right about her too, for at the end of his days, when he had to leave the cottage for the hospital, she brought huge bunches of roses and gladioli from the garden that brought a flicker of life to his eyes and the fragrance of home to the ward. Tony Blair's invitation to Downing Street to the little preteenage girl from Belfast, the one who wrote to him that she had only known one year of peace in her life, surely was driven by the same recognition—that it is not easy to brighten eyes that are making up for lost time. It can make a hard man of you. So it can.

The second Billy represents another and a very different generation in Northern Ireland. He too has the look of a man who has done too much time, like dozens of nationalists and loyalists left in the Maze. It is the summer of 1997, we do not know what decision the Labor government, the Royal Ulster Constabulary police chief, and the secretary of state, Mo Mowlam, are going to make about the Garvaghy Road, and whether the Orangemen will be allowed to march along it on their way back from Drumcree Church. The proposal to grant the Orangemen permission to march based on their legal rights and then to encourage them to forgo that right for the sake of a higher moral road had about as much appeal as a wet bonfire on the Eleventh Night. But Billy has little or no interest in the news in the background as we sit and talk over a cup of tea, the somber mood on the news lightened only by his question—did I know that all three of Mowlam's three sisters were moving to the province? I did not know that, nor that their names were Eeenie, Meenie, and Miney. I even fell for the assertion that he had a very soft spot for his mother-in-law—the Bog Meadows. It is coming up on eleven o'clock and the people of Garvaghy Road still don't know what the decision is.

Billy tells me that he was given three sentences to run concurrently, two for six years and one for three. In all he served seven years in Wing H5, along with twenty-four others in a block that held a hundred inmates during the time in the seventies when they did not separate Ulster Volunteer Force (UVF) and Ulster Defense Association (UDA) men from the Provos. I do not ask him what he did and to whom he had done it, for he has already told me with chilling casualness that he was only in for armed assault. Not like his nationalist cellmate, who had murdered. "He was a hard man," Billy explained, unaware that he himself was about to enter the same canon. "What was so hard about him?" seemed like a logical question. It turned out to include an unflinching hatred of the prison officer (he called him the "screw") during the cell mate's time in solitary confinement, when he—like Billy later—"got a powerful batin'." In fact, the solitary, with its concrete floor and bare walls, seems to have had the same effect on all the inmates, but nothing hardened Billy more than the refusal of a day pass to go to his father's funeral. "But didn't this give you something in common with your cellmate?" I asked in a desperate search for a sign of solidarity, especially as I had just noticed the tattoo on his arm—"Long Kesh"—traced, he said, by his nationalist cellmate with a sewing needle, then dabbed into the skin with ink, dot by dot. "Aye, it did," and then Billy introduced me to a new adverb straight out of the lexicon of the Troubles. "Blockside we got on great. So we did." United in their common hatred of the warden, loyalist and nationalist inmates would give one another "a pack of fags and biscuits." But my thesis of "put them together and they'll get along" crumbled when he added that his cellmate told Billy the day he was released, "Don't you come into my street on the outside or they'll carry you out in a black bin bag."

Billy was released a day earlier than what he had been told—a deliberate ruse, he claims, on the part of prison officials to make life as hard and miserable as they could. No one was there to pick him up. A Provo prisoner released at the same time offered him a lift, which he declined, choosing instead to walk all the way to a loyalist pub in Lisburn, where after seven years of abstinence he got full (falling-down drunk), before heading for home in a black taxi. Yet even after several years on the outside, Billy remains cautious, at least with me. He does not divulge the name of the most notorious loyalist prisoner of the seventies. "I forget his flippin' name." To my question "Was he a hard man, like your cellmate?" the answer was prompt: "No, he was just evil." Apparently, this man had a lot of power outside that he continued to wield, intimidating everybody who crossed him "inside." He had been in and out of the Maze for years, had gotten out on his own recognizance for eighteen months, and then had beaten the charge. He might have been safer inside, for during one of his longer remands he was shot by the Provos. Then the conversation slips out of control, with anecdotes about girlfriends smuggling in rat poison in knickers, inmates slipping it into the tea of one of the screws while they were watching a movie. It is hard to get back on track, and Billy rarely glances at the on-going local newscast about the talks in Hillsborough. The other men at the kitchen table explain to me the difference in the mentality of the UDA and the UVF. They agree that the UVF is filled with men who are after revenge for relatives who have been shot. They tell me about a Protestant farmer who has been in the Maze for years for a revenge shooting, and none of the Catholic farmers for miles around will bid on his cows. I know it didn't used to be like that.

Pigeons brought Billy back to ordinary living, for nothing had been worse on a Saturday afternoon—not even saying goodbye to his widowed mother, who came every week—than to stand outside in the prison yard and watch the birds on their way home from a race. The fifteen-minute visit from his mother had meant little to him—or the others—he claimed. They were all glad to get back into the cell again, for after a year or so there wasn't much to say. One thing was certain. He would never do it again. It had not been worth it. All he wanted now was to place in a big national long-distance pigeon race, like the one coming up the following week from St. Nazarre in France.

Little did Billy know that he would place very high—with a pied hen of the Sion breed that dropped into Billy's loft in a County Down village, the fret marks of exhaustion etched on her little wings from the long flight across two bodies of water. When the birds were released in France, every pigeon fancier in the United Kingdom knew that it would be a hard race, for it had been a terrible summer and the weather forecast had again been poor, though not bad enough to postpone the race. It had been raining on and off, and the greatest danger for the birds was to be swallowed up by the waves when they flew too close to the sea. They say that the pigeon fanciers in the west of England had tears in their eyes when they first spotted the Irish birds. They knew them by the direction they were headed—flying toward home straight into a harsh north wind. And theirs already landed, safe in the nest.

13
France: The Actual
Country

The most surprising aspect about landing in France was the discovery that it was an actual place and not a figment of Miss Crone's imagination. There it was, lying on the horizon at an angle created largely by spectacular seasickness on the way over from Dover, a sea crossing that made the journey the night before from Belfast to Heysham like a boat ride up the Horicon Marsh in Dodge County, Wisconsin.

The Normandy landings in the summer of 1944 are not the only ones; try landing in France with a vocabulary notebook listing the French for garden tools and a stomach stretched like an elastic band from retching between the outer shores of the Isle of Man and Calais, and you will correct your own perspective. It was misery. Nor would they stop using their wretched language on the boat and train, in the face of my obvious suffering. I still notice that phenomenon in life. In the midst of your deepest pain and disappointment, people actually continue to talk and even laugh, acting like your mother hadn't really died at all, the your elderly uncle had not really been robbed and beaten up in his house at the Twelve Arches. You would think at times that everybody travels on stabilized ships in a first-class cabin, with a cup of tea and white toast served first thing in the morning, and that there is no such part of a ship as steerage. And then the crippling recognition, reached before the train had even approached Arras, that the language so assiduously memorized and performed in the front row of Miss Crone's classroom was useless. It might not even be French at all.

The appearance of the train attendants didn't exactly help. They had such an official air about them that it would have intimidated the queen of England. Is there any more effective form of intimidation than to have your third-class rail ticket questioned for its validity? Mine was not, but that's precisely my point. In fact, the train conductor didn't even suggest that the ticket that my mother had purchased for me in Belfast was fake, but everything about him—the vaguely Central European customs officer look, the clipped mustache, the cap, and the uniform—had the effect of depleting years of confidence acquired from parsing verbs and replacing it with a terror of Kafkaesque proportions that threw my whole existence into limbo, at least until I had enough courage to get off the train at the Gare du Nord, where Chantal and her father were waiting for me.

My affection for France began that day on the local train out to Villeneuve St. Georges, and all the goblins of fear—that I did not have a valid ticket to take me anywhere—were chased away by sheer kindness. Although Chantal's father did not speak a word of English, he understood exactly what I needed to learn and even what I wanted to say. I would go with him in the evenings to his allotment, where he grew the best radishes I have ever eaten. Recently, when I sampled the first radishes of my own crop, I could have cried, thinking of the ones I used to eat on the allotment in Villeneuve St. Georges. Mine looked like turnips, were fibrous and bitter, streaked with brown sinews that would have brought tears to a stone. Monsieur Pontviannes's can only be described as luscious. We dipped them in salt and creamy butter and Monsieur Pontvianne would encourage me with the words, "Il faut manger"—You have to eat—I needed little encouragement to eat for I tucked into everything that didn't move.

I had, of course, no idea at the time that I was approaching France by way of its back roads, which led to allotments with radishes dipped in salt and butter rather than the crudités typically offered to visitors. I am aware that radishes are also grown on large estates near Bordeaux and are eaten by people with several *de*'s in their name, but I suspect that radishes with butter are not the first fruits of the soil offered by the French to those who want to learn all about their culture.

I also learned (again in retrospect) that I had fallen into the pace of the people who invited me there and that other people, other French people, did not walk, talk, or eat that way. That first visit prepared me for a job up the road when I taught English to the children of an aristocratic family, in exchange for board and lodgings, a small salary, and the chance to use French at the dinner table. I had to learn a different pace in that environment, but I never forgot the introductory lesson. Nothing bothered me during that first visit to France, and I was never scared, although I was a young teenager abroad for the first time. For a month I learned to walk slowly along the tree-lined street to the train station where I caught the train to Paris, conserving energy just like the French did when it was hot, keeping my eyes averted on the metro when undesirables moved too close, just like Chantal and her parents had told me.

And what a town this Paris was, with its fancy names for the most ordinary things, like café au lait, which turned out to be no different than the milky coffee in White's in Belfast, except that they didn't use White's big urn with shovel-length levers that were pulled down to emit frothy coffee into the waiting cups. I have noticed that hairdressers and smaller restaurants often insert a French accent to perk the place up a bit—like the donut shop in Milwaukee that wisely called itself "Lé Donut." "The Donut" and "White's" just don't cut it as names, and café au lait inserts an ingredient into a cup that "milky coffee" doesn't have. Beyond the sheer sound of these delicacies, however, there was a magic about the place that, with all due respect to Mademoiselle, Bruges and Belfast simply didn't have. First of all, it looked like nobody ever did a hand's turn, what with full-grown men lounging around in broad daylight in open air cafés on boulevards that you could park a combine harvester on, and women who did not look like they had earned the right to have afternoon tea after a long afternoon of shopping in cut-rate shops. These women barely had a basket between them. I am not censuring the French with these remarks, or suggesting that they should have been baling hay, but it did strike me at the time that they looked like a lazy lot. I no longer think so, having joined them once too often at the table.

I was to discover the south of France much later, as an adult, on two very different levels, the first on a visit to the little village of St. Tulle in Haute Provence, where Chantal and her husband had moved some years before. I was already acquainted with the region and its robust women through the eyes of the novelist Jean Giono, but even Giono had not prepared me for the fragrance of the lavender or for the little villages that clung to the hills like wasps' nests. This area was not that far from *Lettres de mon Moulin* country but far more tangible and fragrant than Daudet's landscape. Or could it be that I have been prejudiced by what Daudet's son said in the thirties about taking in foreign refugees? He issued a warning that the French should be careful, otherwise these foreign Jews—many of them refugees from the Third Reich—would end up supporting Germany if a war broke out between the two nations. He was right about support, except that it came from some of his own people.

But I didn't know about French support for the Nazis on the evening when we drove to meet Chantal's friends, two elderly sisters who lived in a tiny village farther up the hillside. No one on the twisted road below could possibly have suspected that a village existed there. The two women greeted us at the door of the farmhouse without surprise, having known Chantal for several years. A woman who sought and valued solitude, Chantal had driven up to the little hamlet out of curiosity one day and apparently over the years had come to be accepted by the few families who lived there. Chantal had been particularly fond of the little thatched cottage up our old lane where Rob Cammock lived, so it was no surprise to me when she drove me to this little village where Rob and his cottage would easily have felt at home. A pot on the open hearth emitted the most delicious aroma of a stew—a daube that presumably would be later eaten for dinner. In the house next door an artist called Serge Fiorio was standing in front of an easel, working on a canvas that captured the amber and gold hues of the deepening twilight in the valley below. I told him so, to which he replied simply, "Je peins ce que je vois" (I paint what I see).

The comment stuck, and I retrieved it later from my memory when I first viewed the art of the Nazi concentration camp at Theresienstadt. Some artists interned there refused to paint propaganda art that depicted the camp favorably. They painted secretly at night and hid their work in the floorboards. But one day their clandestine art was discovered and they were sent off to the Little Fortress up the road from the camp, where their fingers were mutilated—for painting what they saw. One artist was shot, but his paintings were later rescued and tell a dreadful story of what the camp really looked like.

But on that visit to France in the early seventies, I did not even know that there had been an internment camp in Provence at Les Milles, where famous German-Jewish writers like Lion Feuchtwanger and the dramatist Walter Hasenclever had been interned, the latter taking his own life in the camp. Nor did I know that the writer Jean Giono was rumored to be sympathetic toward fascism. For that first visit to St. Tulle and the little villages that surround it was primarily a discovery of the south—Le Midi—and the realization that there is a level of living in the south of France that eludes the most assiduous tourist, and that sun, olives, and lavender have hiding places that the French can scarcely find. And yet without the training in the first row of the French class at Princess Gardens School in Irlande du Nord, I never would have found the way to St. Tulle.

The next level of my discovery of France as an actual country does not obliterate the others, but it blunts my tendency to adulate the place. In many ways I wish I had never heard of Les Milles or Gurs or Noé, for then I could just keep on eating radishes with butter or stay seated in front of the fragrant Provencal farmhouse and pretend that Daudet didn't really mean what he said about the refugees, that Maurice Papon really did cry when he saw the Jews get on the trains that would take them to their deaths, that Kurt's mother hadn't really ended up in Auschwitz.

I met Kurt in Alfortville, on the outskirts of Paris in the summer of 1996, having first read about him in the *Herald Tribune.* An Austrian-born Jew, he was challenging the French government to release all the documents that had been embargoed during and after the war. I was working on a research project, investigating the representation of the German-Jewish experience in Vichy France. In my notes I called him "Monsieur S.," like an appropriate informant. What I did not expect was an Austrian. Yet who was I to insist on a Frenchman, just because he had lived in France since the midthirties and spoke—at least it sounded that way to me—like a Frenchman? Furthermore, he called his cat his son—"mon fils"—and scolded it for being naughty. We spoke in German. We spoke about Vichy France in German. Monsieur S. told me in a lengthy face-to-face conversation what I had read about in the newspapers—that he had gone to the archives in Toulouse to find more information about his parents, both of whom had perished in Auschwitz. The family had emigrated from Vienna in the midthirties to France, where Kurt had joined the Foreign Legion. Both parents had been arrested in one of the notorious *rafles,* the roundups of Jews that happened under German Occupation, carried out for the most part by French police and without German help.

Kurt spent the last year of the war in hiding, and when he returned to his former home, he learned that his parents had last been seen in one of the internment camps in the Unoccupied Zone—the so-called Free Zone. From there—the camp at Noé—they had been sent to an "unknown destination." They were among the thousands of foreign-born and native-born Jews who had been transported from France. In all, seventy-six thousand had perished. Why had he waited until the early nineties to find out more about the last days of his parents? The convoluted answer suggested that I should never have asked. We were talking over dinner in an Armenian restaurant in Alfortville, drinking buttermilk, which I had not tasted since my childhood in Northern Ireland, talking in German about what it was like to be a German-speaking Jewish emigrant in 1935 in France. I was in the process of attempting to understand how that experience had been represented in the works of famous German-Jewish writers, like Franz Werfel (the author of *The Song of Bernadette*) and Anna Seghers. I knew that the German-Jewish philosopher Walter Benjamin had taken his own life while trying to get out of France. In frail health he had managed to get over the Pyrenees, but when he was turned back on the Spanish side, Benjamin took an overdose of pills, rather than face an uncertain fate by going back to France.

My interest in the subject of representation of experience, however, had been gradually drawn to other narratives, by people who were not famous. I was coming to the conclusion that fictional or semifictional accounts were removed from depicted events by more than literary devices. For example, diaries written in internment camps or in hiding portrayed a much sharper sense of political reality than their literary counterparts, a much more sober evaluation of the consequences and effects of the German Occupation of France on the Jewish population. This was one issue I wanted to talk about with Monsieur S. But he wanted to talk about his mother. He told me that when the photo of his mother fell out of the folder in the Toulouse archive in 1990, he was transfixed. He stole the photo of his mother. He was later accused of stealing other documents—actually several thousand—which he secretly photocopied with the collaboration of an archivist. Kurt insists he *stole* only one—the photo of his mother.

Meeting Kurt both connected me to and disconnected me from France. As I made my way out to Alfortville to meet him, it was like returning to the little *banlieu* of Villeneuve St. Georges, which was surprisingly near—the same unhurried pace, the tree-lined streets, the wonderful intermingled smells of garlic-laced cooking and colognes. Monsieur Pontvianne had teased me as a teenager about a German student, a young man who had been in class with me. I can't even remember his name. One day he had walked with me to the metro, where I often met Chantal at the end of my school day. On returning home, Chantal told her parents that a good-looking little German boy—"un petit allemand, un beau garçon"—had accompanied me to the metro. I was mortified for, frankly, I thought he was a bit of a drip. But the incident stuck, especially with Monsieur Pontvianne, and whenever I was late coming home, he invariably concluded, with undisguised sarcasm, that I was with the lovely little German boy. I had unwittingly been the instigator that triggered all sorts of unpleasant connections for Monsieur Pontvianne, whose past still haunted him—all because of a harmless encounter with a German boy who was as keen to learn French as I was.

In the course of one of our excursions to the allotment, Monsieur Pontvianne launched into a long story about the war and how the French had to go off and work in the German Reich. Thousands of French had worked all over the Reich. I wish I could remember whether he himself had gone, but it seems to me that, by the way he was going on, half of Villeneuve St. Georges worked in Germany, so I suspect he was one of them. He probably called the Germans *les boches* but I did not know then what I know now, otherwise I might have eaten fewer radishes and asked more questions.

One thing is certain—I too would have stolen a photo if I had been looking for signs of what became of my mother, especially if she were heading for an unknown destination. My mother had prepared me well to go to places beyond Belfast. Her favorite maxim was "Take an interest in everybody you meet and everything you see." And so I tend to see the mothers of other people through the lens of my own mother. I cannot imagine the burden of knowing that my mother had been sent to an unknown destination. What would you take an interest in on such a journey? It was stressful to make my way as a teenager from Belfast to the known destination of France. I still remember the anxiety in the pit of my stomach. But the memory is now deeply undergirded by the confidence that Chantal and her family are there to welcome me in France. My journey as a teenager led me to more than a destination but to an actual French family that embraced me and my family in County Down. Chantal mourned when our parents died, just as we did the day she phoned to tell us about the death of her father.

It's the unknown destinations that are the killers. No wonder Kurt picked up that photo of his mother from the floor. I would have too, and so fast that no one would have noticed me bend. He must have seen her whole life compressed on that last photo—not a tag of identification that now belonged to an archive file but the remains of a life that belonged to him. I doubt he was thinking at that moment about how France had not protected his mother from deportation during the Dark Years. But surely how a country treats your mother tells as much as you need to know about its soul or the lack of one—even if the place where its heart used to be is just temporarily occupied.

14

Elegy in a Jewish Graveyard

It is high summer, 1994. Computer disks and numerous files and folders have long since replaced the green Princess Gardens School notebooks. My vocabulary now embraces words that would do Miss Crone proud. I am a guest professor in Gießen, teaching the literature of exile that was written by Germans and Austrians who fled after Hitler came to power. The prospect of a long weekend in Bavaria offers a welcome reprieve from the scrutiny of young Germans, who know surprisingly little about the fate of writers—most of them Jews—who had to flee from the Nazi Reich in the thirties. I am working hard to earn their respect. Despite my surname, it helps that I am not German. They are more interested in my native roots in Northern Ireland than my years in the United States. Anna Seghers's short story *Der Ausflug der toten Mädchen* (The Excursion of the Dead Girls) finally breaks the ice, and they begin to talk about the burden of their legacy, reluctantly handed down from their parents, who had dealt with even worse—the silence of their grandparents. They were clearly moved by the power of the Seghers story, which connected them to a past that was a painful part of their heritage.

As we drive though the narrow streets of Harburg, the smell of cow dung hangs unequivocally in the air. We—my husband and I—are heading for a farm located at the far end of the village where Mr. T. is expecting us and will lead us to the Jewish cemetery. He will climb up on an ancient tractor that looks to me like the old Massey Ferguson we had in Ballycoan, and we will follow him up into the hills that surround Harburg. Just a few minutes before, we had turned off the Romantische Straße, the famous road with gentle curves and gracefully undulating hills that bears the daily burden of luxury coaches headed for Munich with tourists who have already stopped for coffee or lunch in fragrant little Dinkelsbühl or Rothenburg ob der Taube. I do not suppose they will stop in Harburg.

Dung is fundamentally dung, but the Bavarian variety strikes a nose seasoned on a County Down farm as particularly pungent, and it's not hard to work out why: Dung enjoys an astonishing degree of freedom in this part of the world and is permitted to ferment right under the apron of the town on farms like Mr. T.'s, as opposed to wafting half-baked in the open countryside over hawthorn hedgerows, diluted by every breeze that wanders by. Mr. T. does not know that I hold these views, nor that I am observing his hands and am poised to impose yet another obsessive connection, namely, that his fingers look just as swollen and cracked as their North Irish counterparts from working with cows' tough hindquarters. He is Willie John with a Bavarian accent. The Massey-Ferguson struggles up the sharp incline, giving us ample time to look back at the receding profile of Harburg, the castle of the Oettingen-Wallerstein family imperiously etched on the steep hill, its presence, though now symbolic, a dramatic reminder of the power structure that shaped these picturesque little Bavarian farm towns. (And we thought Irwin the landlord had power.)

A car is parked at the side of the walled graveyard, which Mr. T. explains belongs to Mr. H., who has been working on the restoration of the gravestones for some time and would certainly be glad to meet someone involved in Jewish Studies. There we stand — the Bavarian farmer, probably now in his seventies, whose father and grandfather had tended this same cemetery and had performed sabbath chores for local Jewish farmers; the journalist Mr. H., who had sought out healthier air than his native Stuttgart offered and now, as one of the few Jews in the area, is writing articles for the *Donauwörther Zeitung* about the former Jewish community in Harburg; and my husband and I, who just the night before had first heard about Harburg's Jewish cemetery at the choir picnic of Ehlingen Lutheran Church.

This is how we ended up at a church picnic. It was early evening by the time we finally located the tiny hamlet of Schopflohe, where my husband's great-great grandfather, Franz Hanser, had been the minister of the local Lutheran church. We had thought that we were looking for Schop*floch,* which would have satisfied another desire to visit the place. A Jewish colleague whose ancestors came from there had told me a fascinating story: Two hundred years ago in Schopfloch Lutheran cattle dealers joined with Jewish cattle dealers to protect both themselves and one another against the unfair business practices of cattle dealers from other farming communities in the area. Together they developed a Hebrew-based language called Lachoudisch, which they used during business deals to communicate with each other. The language survived even the Third Reich and is spoken today by several people in the little town, including the mayor. But Schopfloch expelled its Jewish population in the thirties. A common language and a love for cattle were not enough to confront an ideology that stripped Jews of their right to be farmers, of their right to be Germans, and ultimately of their right to live. I had even been able to meet the mayor, briefly, as it turned out—I should have made an appointment, he pointed out firmly—but yes, the church would have a list of former ministers that went back several centuries. But there were no Hansers on the list that I carefully scrutinized in the parsonage office—for which I was grateful, when my eyes later fell on the mural at the front of the church, which depicts Jesus and his disciples as blond Aryans and was painted in 1935. Maybe we should try another place called Schopf-*lohe,* the pastor suggested. It was about fifty kilometers away. I asked him whether the mural was an insult to both Jews and Christians. "It's history," he replied.

So it was with a certain weariness and few expectations that we pulled up in the little farm village of Schopflohe. The first person we met was a woman by the name of Reichardt, who was watering geraniums on her husband's grave (he had fallen over dead in his early forties, she later explained). She was able to tell us that the pastor had the only key to the church, but he lived in Ehlingen, where he also was pastor of another small Lutheran congregation. But, then, maybe the organist had a key, and she would gladly drive with us the five hundred yards or so up the village to his farm.

Nothing was a bother to the amiable Frau Reichardt, who brightened at the mention of Franz Hanser and knew there were both a photo of Franz Hanser and a chronicle written by him inside the church. But first she removed her headscarf before setting off for the two-minute drive to the organist's, who in fact did not have a key but knew that the pastor at that very hour was attending the annual Ehlingen Lutheran Church Choir picnic. But first he must change out of his farm clothes and only then were we on our way to the choir picnic, but not before we had driven Mrs. Reichardt back to the watering can waiting by the grave of her late husband, whose biography had meanwhile grown, especially during the time the organist was changing his clothes. Herr Reichardt had been married before and had brought several children into the second marriage with Frau Reichardt, who had loved them all but especially the boy who had died of a disease that eluded me in the middle of a fiercely Bavarian consonant cluster. By now I would have gladly stayed with Frau Reichardt and helped her water the flowers, except I would probably have to change into working clothes.

Within ten minutes we were in a field near Ehlingen, two people who could barely hold a tune, invited by the minister to partake at the high table of Ehlingen Church Choir alongside the choir director, a dairy farmer when he was not singing. Choir offspring played in a sand pile that had been dumped on the grass for the occasion, the sun was now sinking on the heels of a hot day, and the *craic* was good, sweetened by a Bavarian dialect that rolled its *Freilichs* (of courses) halfway up the country and back. We were welcome guests, for after all we were related to Pastor Franz Hanser, whose photo and chronicle were in the church office, and the Reverend T. would return with us in tow to the little church (*Ja, freilich*) after we had finished eating, and then he would come back for the postpicnic activities.

Indeed, apart from the incongruity of an imported sand pile, the event could have been a belated wake for Franz Hanser, not in the "celebrate his life" sense but as an occasion to tuck into a hearty meal in a field with Franz's friends. There would, of course, have been more reverent reflection had we known at the picnic/wake of how he had found the strength to cope with rearing a brood of motherless children after his wife died in childbirth; and the frustration of having to defend his support of the 1848 political uprisings would certainly have drawn from us a respectful comment. We did not ask the present choir director if he supported Franz Hanser's political views, for after all it was 1994 and we would not learn about Franz's position toward 1848 till later, in the back office of the church in Schopflohe. For now it was enough to tell at high table what we did know—that Franz Hanser's son Otto had emigrated to America and Otto's granddaughter married a Lutheran pastor from Wisconsin and ended up in a town called Horicon. Surely, this kinship gave us as much right as any Bavarian, Lutheran or not, to be present on this balmy July evening in 1994.

The children, long since bored with the sand pile, were now chasing one another up and down the field. Besides, who better to talk to than German dairy farmers about the price of milk in Northern Ireland? Sooner or later the conversation would drift to where I had learned to speak German, a harmless enough inquiry as long as it stayed in Belfast, but ultimately the conversation found its way beyond Belfast to my area of research on the Holocaust. The word fell on the Ehlingen Church Choir picnic like a zeppelin, rescued only by the young pastor's hearty suggestion that I meet his father, who tended the Jewish cemetery in Harburg, just a few miles away from the Romantische Straße. It would not take us out of the way to our destination of Munich—actually, the archives at Dachau. I refrained from giving the specific destination.

And that's how we came to be standing the next

morning with Mr. T. and Mr. H. in the Jewish cemetery in Harburg, after spending the night in Nördlingen. The minister had phoned his father when he got home from the picnic, and now the elderly man was expecting us. We stood for a long time, the German Jew and the North Irish woman, while my American husband wandered off with Mr. T. among the graves, gamely trying to speak German. The journalist and I, however, were already talking with the particular kind of intensity that comes from working for years with documents on people whose lives have become part of one's own. There had been a flourishing Jewish community in the eighteenth and nineteenth centuries in Harburg, I learned. After days of scrubbing and rubbing, the names on the gravestones were appearing under Mr. H.'s persistent hands. He was visibly disappointed that I could not help him decipher the Hebrew inscriptions.

After I returned to Wisconsin, I received copies of four articles that Mr. H. had written for the *Donauwörther Zeitung*, describing the lives of people like Isaac Stein, who was born in 1877 in Harburg, studied in Berlin, and in 1902 wrote his doctoral dissertation, "The Jews in the Swabian Imperial Cities During the Reign of King Sigmund, 1410–37." By the time he was twenty-seven, Stein was the district rabbi of Memel. He died in Berlin in 1915 of kidney failure and was buried in Harburg, with rabbis in attendance from Ansbach and Tilsit. His grave has vanished. Raphael

Mai was also born in Harburg (in 1806), studied medicine at the University of Würzburg, and, after being licensed to practice medicine in Munich, returned to Harburg to take care of the workers when the railway was built between 1845 and 1850. The mayor of Harburg recommended Dr. Mai for the order of St. Michael after fifty years of devoted service. (The doctor had traced the source of a smallpox epidemic in 1840 to a weaver who had infected his customers.) Sadly, the officials in Augsburg did not agree with the recommendation of the Harburg mayor, but Mr. H. points out in his article that Dr. Mai nonetheless continued with his medical practice, making no difference in his treatment of Jews and Christians. The original of the letter outlining the refusal is in the archives of the Oettingen-Wallerstein Castle in Harburg.

Then there was the Guldmann family, which lived in Harburg for two hundred years, starting with Lämle Alexander, who was given permission to reside in Harburg in 1745—*Schutzaufnahme* (a protective measure) in German. The butcher, Hajum Hirsch Guldmann, spent his whole life in Harburg from 1804 until 1886. His son Leopold emigrated to the United States in 1870 (about the time that Otto Hanser left Schopflohe) and arrived in New York on the *Cimbria*. Leopold headed for Watertown, Wisconsin, and spent seven years working in a department store before ending up in Colorado, where he founded the Golden Eagle Dry advisers did not tell him to keep on driving past Bitburg and head for the little cemetery in Harburg.

You would think that I would have asked Mr. H. what happened after 1933, but I didn't, for I already knew the answer. The German poet Ilse Blumenthal-Weiss, a survivor of the Holocaust, once said that she wanted to write about the sun but the night kept breaking through. It was so peaceful that day up on the Hühnerberg. Its peacefulness captivated me for a brief moment and inserted temporary parentheses in the German-Jewish relationship, which was forged as much by the rough hands of the Lutheran farmer as the persistent hands of the Jewish journalist. Theirs is a silent unsung partnership that insists on a life that once was and that must be preserved by rubbing and scrubbing until the names are coaxed back into the light. Mr. H. later wrote that the gravestones (and I translate) "have turned out unexpectedly beautiful." He has still two more articles to send me, the second of which will deal directly with the graveyard up on the Hühnerberg. God willing, I'll write about that later. So I will.

Irish Studies in Literature and Culture